ENDORSEMENTS BY PASTORS

"David Peter's observations and prescriptions soundly resonate with my experiences as a pastor in the three midsize congregations I have served. While there are plenty of books that criticize the church, this book builds up, helps out, and is honest about the hybrid nature of ministry in midsize churches. This book is a valuable, informed, and long over-due contribution. Any leader who desires to understand the dynamics at play in a midsize church needs to spend time with this immensely practical resource!"

—Rev. Dr. Matthew Henry,
Senior Pastor,
Friendship Celebration Church, Meridian, ID

"Dr. Peter accurately examines, affirms, and celebrates the unique identity, dynamics, challenges, and opportunities of the midsize congregation with thoughtful, theological, practical, and gospel-centered insights. This work is a must-read for every leader of a midsize congregation who is seeking to serve Christ effectively within their distinctive context."

—Rev. Dr. Matthew Bean,
Senior Pastor,
Redeemer Lutheran Church, Richmond, VA

"In a sea of books on church ministry, few attend to the distinct opportu-nities and challenges related to church size. David Peter has addressed this oversight with an insightful and thorough treatment of leading midsize churches. I pray that this book gains a wide audience and leads to more fruitful ministry. Read with pen in hand!"

—Rev. Dr. W. Jackson Watts,
Pastor,
Grace Free Will Baptist Church, Arnold, MO

"So many materials are written for small, or more likely larger, congre-gations, that they don't spend significant time addressing the particular issues midsize churches face. This makes it difficult for pastors like me to synthesize bits and pieces of seven to eight different books in ways that the average congregational member can understand. Here is one resource that I can actually put in the hands of my laypeople to help them understand that our church is not broken or struggling, it is going through the quite normal transitions of any church our size."

—Rev. Dr. Chris Ascher,
Pastor,
Resurrection Lutheran Church, Sioux Falls, SD

ENDORSEMENTS BY SCHOLARS AND LEADERS

"Lyle Schaller, the eminent ecclesial sage of the latter twentieth century, viewed the midsize church as rather unpredictable, at times even volatile. David Peter's *Maximizing the Midsize Church* demystifies the complexities of these 75,000+ congregations, providing compelling insights and best practices for leveraging mission. Many comparable texts miss the 'why' of impactful witness. Peter wonderfully moves the reader from analyst to change agent, calling the best out of God's people for the sake of the gospel. Be encouraged as you apply the wisdom of this considerable resource!"

—Dr. Thomas F. Tumblin,
Professor of Leadership,
Asbury Theological Seminary

"David Peter takes up an important question. There are many books on small churches and especially those that want us to envy the big churches. But Peter asks how to maximize the medium-sized church as it is. That does not mean making it large. It means maximizing the ways that its people experience the love of Christ."

—Dr. Scott Cormode,
Hugh De Pree Professor of Leadership Development,
Fuller Theological Seminary, Pasadena, CA

"With a pastor's seasoned perspective, scholarly insight, and engaging style, David Peter unfolds the challenges and opportunities of the midsize church. Providing both a deep understanding of the medium-sized church's identity and a clear grasp of its direction, *Maximizing the Midsize Church* offers sound and actionable wisdom for staffing, ministry efforts, and mission focus. This book will bring clarity, blessing, and direction to church professionals and lay leaders alike."

—Rev. Michael W. Newman,
Author of *Gospel DNA: Five Markers of a Flourishing Church*

"David Peter has crafted a gem for every leader of a midsize church. He knows it. He's led it. He's studied it. He's taught aspiring pastors about it. There's enormous downward pressure on all churches in our increasingly secularized culture today. The midsize church is no different. I recommend this book to you! You'll gain insights. You'll make sense of things that don't make sense. And—when everything else escapes you—David will encourage you and your congregation and remind you to focus on the mission!"

—Rev. Dr. Jock Ficken,
Co-Executive Leader, Pastoral Leadership Institute

"For the 75,000 midsize congregations in the US that experience weekly worship attendance between 150 and 400 worshipers, professor and practitioner David Peter provides a very helpful and much needed resource to maximize their potential and make a significant impact for the mission of God in their ministry context. Not only does David identify and diagnose the challenges typically encountered in the midsize congregation, he provides useful best practices for leading the midsize congregation and increasing its effectiveness for mission and ministry."

—Rev. Dr. Anthony Steinbronn,
President, New Jersey District, LCMS

"As a middle child who spent twenty-four years in a midsize congregation, I really appreciated Dr. David Peter's *Maximizing the Midsize Church: Effective Leadership for Fruitful Mission and Ministry*. The midsize congregation is neglected in the literature of church administration. Dr. Peter shows that he understands and appreciates what many of us have experienced in serving midsize congregations. I wish I could have read chapter 8 on dealing with personnel twenty-five years ago! This chapter alone makes the book worth reading. He introduces each chapter with a true-to-life vignette that connects the subject with the reader in a personal way. What I appreciated most was Dr. Peter's consistent affirmation of what it means to be a pastor, a leader, or a member of a midsize congregation. We all know the perils of serving in a midsize congregation. It was great to hear the promises and possibilities! I will certainly be encouraging pastors to read it."

—Rev. Dr. Steven Turner,
President, Iowa District West, LCMS

"As a member and lay leader in a midsize church, I recommend this book to the pastor, leaders, professional staff, and laity of any midsize church. The author provides a mirror by which you can examine your own church and your role and participation in the programmatic aspects of the church. After reading this book, I found myself more excited and energized about the possibilities for my church to thrive as it carries out God's mission."

—Karen Soeken,
Member,
Our Savior Lutheran Church, Laurel, MD

MAXIMIZING
THE MIDSIZE CHURCH

EFFECTIVE LEADERSHIP FOR
FRUITFUL MISSION AND MINISTRY

DAVID J. PETER

Maximizing the Midsize Church: Effective Leadership for Fruitful Mission and Ministry

© 2018 David J. Peter

Published by Kregel Ministry, an imprint of Kregel Publications, 2450 Oak Industrial Dr. NE, Grand Rapids, MI 49505.

ISBN 978–0–8254–4565–1

Printed in the United States of America

18 19 20 21 22 / 5 4 3 2 1

To my wife, Tonya, whose name means "priceless."
You are a precious gift of God and I treasure
our love and life together.

"An excellent wife who can find?
She is far more precious than jewels."
—Proverbs 31:10

CONTENTS

ACKNOWLEDGMENTS

I am indebted to many for their contributions to this book. I have received tremendous insight from serving two medium-sized congregations—Trinity Lutheran Church in Peoria, Illinois, and Messiah Lutheran Church in St. Louis, Missouri. These experiences have helped me understand the practical realities of ministry in the midsize context.

As a seminary professor I have integrated the study of the social dynamics of congregational size into courses that I teach. In discussions with students, particularly doctoral students who serve congregations, I have gained significant insights about the workings of the midsize church. In addition, I have led summer continuing education events entitled "Help for the Midsize Church," attended by numerous pastoral and lay leaders. From these practitioners of ministry—participants in the seminary classes and the continuing education workshops—I have learned enormously. Many of the insights and best practices in this book derive from their contributions.

I am grateful to Concordia Seminary for granting me a sabbatical to begin the research and writing for this book. My thanks goes to Chris Ascher, Gillian Bond, Kendall Davis, Benjamin Haupt, and Jedidiah Maschke, who read drafts and provided helpful recommendations for revision. Their insights sharpened this material, but they are not responsible for its content.

INTRODUCTION

Not uncommonly, those in the middle get overlooked. Middle-born children are often not given the same amount of attention in the family as their oldest and youngest siblings. States in the central part of the country are regarded as flyover zones. Advertisers pay the least attention to the middle-age demographic. Economically, the middle class is getting squeezed out. In politics, the far right or far left silences the centrists. Folks in the middle oftentimes appear invisible.

Something similar has happened to middle-sized churches. They receive relatively little attention from church analysts, consultants, and publishers. In my research for this book I conducted a bibliographic search in the library of the seminary at which I teach. I discovered an entire shelf containing dozens of books devoted to leading the small church. The number of books focusing on large churches filled a smaller section of another shelf, yet it was substantial. However, there was only one book dedicated exclusively to the midsize church, and it was published in 1985, over thirty years ago. Apparently medium-size congregations fit the phenomenon of the neglected middle.

This book undertakes to address that oversight. It provides a comprehensive analysis of midsize congregations and significant resources for their pastors and leaders. Medium churches have the potential to make significant impact for the mission of God. The purpose of this book is to maximize the fruitfulness of these parishes both for the Lord's kingdom and for his glory.

A preview of the book's subject matter provides an initial vision of the purpose, scope, and development of its content. The first four chapters focus on how the midsize church is distinct from other-sized congregations, specifically small and large congregations. These chapters identify cultural characteristics and dynamics that are distinctive of the church with an average worship attendance of 150 to 400 people. They diagnose problems that are typically encountered in the midsize congregation and promote opportunities for flourishing.

Chapter 5 articulates the evangelical priorities to which leaders and members of the midsize church should aspire. These are determined by Scripture and directive for practice. This provides a theological center for carrying out mission and ministry in the medium church. It essentially identifies *what* the church should be doing and *why* it is to do so.

The final five chapters provide guidance on *how* to carry out God's priorities in the middle-sized parish in several critical areas of congregational ministry. This is the most comprehensive section of the book and provides useful best practices for leading the midsize congregation in developing healthy programs, cultivating effective pastoral leadership, forming a staff team, recruiting and equipping lay volunteer leaders, and maximizing overall productivity.[1]

A postscript is appended that identifies resources for navigating the transition of a medium congregation to a large church or a small one.

Lastly, the reader is alerted to the use of gender in personal pronouns. When referring to a person in general terms only one gender is given in any instance. For example, *she* is utilized instead of *he/she, she/he, she or he,* or other similar combinations. Thus in odd-numbered chapters masculine pronouns are consistently employed (i.e., he, him, his). In even-numbered chapters feminine pronouns are used (i.e., she, her, hers). This alternation in the gender of pronouns is intended to communicate inclusivity and avoid awkward construction.

---

1. Throughout this book the terms *lay* and *laypeople* will be used. These refer to members of a church who are not professional church workers. This usage in no way endorses a class system or hierarchical view that elevates clergy and church staff as having more value or status than others in the church. I strongly affirm the doctrine of the priesthood of all believers and regard all Christians as having an equal standing before God whose gifts and service are to be equally valued. The usage of these terms is to clarify distinctions in roles, not to differentiate value or status, using conventional terminology for communicating a distinction that Scripture itself makes (see Eph. 4:11–12, Phil. 1:1–2, 1 Tim. 3:1–13, Titus 1:5–9, 1 Peter 5:1–3).

CHAPTER 1

PURPOSE

Gordon fumed to himself, "If we please one, we displease the other!" He had just concluded an intense conversation with a founding member of Faith Church, Emily. Gordon was also a longtime member of the congregation, and his friendship with Emily spanned several decades. Both had been integrally involved in the life of this church since its earliest years. Both were emotionally invested in the congregation and cared deeply about the church's future direction. But on some matters they didn't see eye to eye. Indeed, the points of contention seemed to multiply with the passing of time.

Gordon was the head elder of the congregation. He had held that role for six years. Previous to being elected the chairperson, he had been a member of the Elders Board for a dozen years. So he knew the workings of the congregation—its issues and challenges. Nevertheless, the pressure of serving in this leadership role was getting to him. The pressure came from two constituencies in the church, each with differing expectations.

EMILY'S LAMENT

On the one side were many of the older and long-term members of the parish. They remembered when Faith Church was smaller in size. At that time the congregation felt to them like one big family. In fact, the founding pastor frequently referred to it as such. "Welcome to the family of faith at Faith Church!" was the way in which he routinely started the Sunday morning worship service thirty-five years ago. That was back when there was only one worship service, not two. Everybody knew each other, and all the members could greet one another at worship. In fact, people in the church did everything together. They shared monthly potlucks together. They decorated the church for Christmas together. The congregational members made decisions about the church at their monthly voters' assemblies. Most of all, they all cared for one another in an organic and intuitive manner.

But that was the past. The church no longer was small enough for everyone to know each other and to care directly for one another. The church had grown, but at a price. Rather than members having a direct voice in the monthly voters' assembly, meetings were held only twice a year to pass the budget and to elect officers. It was the officers of the church council and boards who now made the decisions. A multitude of programs existed at Faith Church—adult education classes, youth group, choirs and instrumental ensembles, children's ministry, missional communities, women's auxiliaries, small groups. This meant that members were associated primarily with niche groups. To Emily and other longtime members, it seemed that Faith Church had become fragmented. She perceived that people were going in many different directions rather than sharing a common life together. "We have lots of interest groups," Emily complained to Gordon, "but little interest in one another as a whole church."

Particularly problematic for Emily, and for others like her, was the fact that the pastor was no longer as available for pastoral care as had been the case in earlier times. He had become more like a manager than a minister, she lamented. As the church had grown it seemed to become more impersonal and atomized. Emily didn't like it, and neither did many of her friends who had joined the church when it was a smaller family-like gathering. So she voiced her frustration to Gordon, whom she respected and felt would listen. She hoped that the head elder, in his leadership role, would share her concerns and work to reverse the direction in which the church was moving. She encouraged him to seek to restore the congregation to its earlier condition as a more personal, intimate, and unified community of faith.

JACK'S AGENDA

But Emily and other like-minded members weren't the only ones Gordon was hearing from. There was also a group of newer members who held a very different vision for Faith Church. This constituency was composed mainly of middle-aged members who had joined the church within the past seven years. The most vocal spokesperson for them was Jack, who also served on the Board of Elders. Jack was in his first term as an elder, and he had ideas for changes to the church that differed greatly from those Emily advocated.

Jack joined Faith Church four years earlier when he had been transferred to the community by his company. Jack was a devoted Christian, passionate about his faith, but his past experience with church had been in one much larger than Faith. That congregation had an average worship attendance of over two thousand, whereas Faith Church's attendance was 240, about one-eighth that size. The large church that Jack had formerly attended provided a cornucopia of ministry opportunities that dwarfed the number of programmatic offerings at Faith Church. Its worship services had a wow factor that Faith's worship venue could never approximate. A small army of specialized staff carried out leadership of the multitude of ministry niches available.

This was Jack's experience of church prior to coming to Faith Church. And this was Jack's vision of what Faith Church could, and should, become. So Jack pushed the pastor and congregational leaders, especially the members of the Elders Board, to learn more about church growth principles and practices. His former church in the other city sponsored an annual four-day conference that commended its model of ministry to attendees. Jack advocated that Faith Church's pastor and congregational officers participate. Furthermore, Jack proposed that they follow each step of the megachurch's prescribed process so that Faith Church would similarly grow in size.

GORDON'S DILEMMA

As a result of the pressures coming from Emily and her ilk on the one hand and Jack and other like-minded members on the other hand, Gordon felt squeezed. The expectations from the two sides were contradictory and contentious. Faith Church, Gordon maintained, was no longer a small church. But neither was it a large congregation as envisioned by Jack. "I guess we are a midsize church," Gordon spoke to himself. "Is that so bad? Is that an unacceptable position to be in? What's wrong with that?"

As a leader in the congregation, Gordon came to realize that he couldn't please either of the parties who contended for the future of Faith Church. But he also recognized that this was not his responsibility. His responsibility was to please God. And that duty wasn't exclusively his; it belonged to the entire congregation. That was Faith Church's purpose—to advance what God had purposed for it to be and to do. Was it possible that the size of the church as it existed today—a medium church—was pleasing to God for that time and place? Was it possible that Faith Church was called to carry out the Lord's work in this community and beyond not as a small congregation, nor as a large assembly, but as a midsize church? If so, how could it maximize efforts toward mission and ministry in a way that most pleased God?

Gordon began to sense that pursuing something that Faith Church wasn't—a small church or a large church—shouldn't be his agenda. God had brought the community of believers at Faith not only for such a *time* as this (Est. 4:14) but also for such a *size* as this. The Lord had called them to be faithful and fruitful in that condition. So Gordon determined to work toward helping Faith Church maximize its positive potential as a midsize church until God saw fit to bring it to a different size.[1]

---

1. The narrative depicting the experiences of leaders of Faith Church continues at the beginning of each succeeding chapter.

PERIMETER PRESSURES

Gordon's dilemma is one that is faced by many lay leaders and pastors in midsize churches—congregations that average between 150 and 400 worshippers each week. Such leaders feel pressure from different sides. They face expectations from the members of their congregations to achieve a congregational culture and ministry conditions that do not fit well with the midsize church. Some want the qualities of a small church with its personal care and intimate relationships among all members. Others want the characteristics of a large church with its myriad of ministry offerings and polished presentation.

Accordingly there is a season of discontent that is endemic to the midsize church. If you are a member or leader of a midsize church perhaps you have experienced this discontentment. You know personally the pressures that accompany it!

JUST RIGHT

A primary presupposition of this book is that God calls many Christian congregations to function in the capacity of medium-sized congregations (averaging 150 to 400 in worshippers per week). God has created a significant number of midsize churches, and he has a purpose for them. In the United States alone, it is estimated that upwards of one-fourth of all congregations fall into this size category, numbering over 75,000 churches.[2] Thus their vocation is to carry out God's mission as midsize churches. This is their place in God's design for the present time. As such, pastors and leaders of those congregations can be content and not pursue becoming something God isn't calling their churches to be. After all, contentment is a Christian virtue (1 Tim. 6:6).

No doubt you are familiar with the children's story about Goldilocks. The young girl wanders into a cottage in the woods that had been occupied by three bears. Goldilocks literally makes herself at home, finding a size portion of some food and the size fit of some furniture to be "just right" for her tastes.

In the scenario presented earlier featuring members of Faith Church, each individual was seeking the size that she or he perceived would be *just right* for the congregation. Emily thought that a small church culture would be *just right*. Jack believed that the characteristics of a large church would be *just right*. But Gordon settled for what God had provided at that time and place—a midsize church. For him, the size of Faith Church was *just right*.

God uses various sizes of Christian congregations to advance his kingdom. God is no respecter of sizes when it comes to churches. "There is no 'best size' for a church," Timothy Keller asserts. "Each size presents

---

2.   This estimate will be documented in chapter two.

great difficulties and also many opportunities for ministry that churches of other sizes cannot undertake (at least not as well). Only together can churches of all sizes be all that Christ wants the church to be."[3] The size that your congregation is right now is the size that God has appointed for it, at least for the time being. The American *zeitgeist* assumes that bigger is better. Some who hold a more romantic view of the church affirm that smaller is better. But neither needs to be the case. Any size of congregation can effectively carry out the mission and ministry that God entrusts to it. And that is true for the middle-sized church as well.

It is hoped that you will see that the size of your church may be *just right* for the work that God calls it to. God has a purpose for creating the congregation to be the size that it is. This is what he has given you to lead at this time and in this place. Instead of pursuing what the church is not, accept what it is, celebrate its uniqueness, and embrace its purpose. Learn to apply the secret of contentment that the Apostle Paul commends (Phil. 4:12).

CONTENT, BUT NOT COMPLACENT   *Cautious Risk*

Indeed, contentment is a virtue for Christians. Yet contentment can also lead to a vice. It becomes problematic when it leads to apathy, complacency, and laziness. This certainly is not God's will for us! It is not the divine purpose for his people! Sinful humans are prone to veer toward sinful extremes. One extreme is for church leaders to fail to be grateful for the context of ministry in which God has placed them; they lack contentment. The opposite extreme is to be like Goldilocks—to become so comfortable in the setting that seems just right that one falls asleep in ministry.

The godly virtue of contentment can be taken to the extreme of complacency, leading to a shirking of responsibility and to the benign neglect of the purposes that God has given to the church. Congregational leaders who adopt such a tack, if they can be called leaders at all, fail to challenge the members of the parish to incarnate the difficult life of discipleship and mission. Ultimately they fail to take up the cross and follow Jesus. As a result, the entire assembly misses the purpose to which it has been called.

Leaders of medium-size churches can find satisfaction in the size context of the congregations they serve. But this distinctive context of being midsize calls for our very best! It calls us to work in ways that are both smart and sanctified. It calls us to learn from the insights and best practices of others who have effectively blazed the trail in leading midsize parishes. This book integrates those learnings into a field guide to help medium congregations navigate the terrain of doing mission and ministry in this challenging era.

---

3. Timothy Keller, *Leadership and Church Size Dynamics: How Strategy Changes with Growth* (New York: Redeemer City to City, 2010), 2.

THE PURPOSE OF THIS BOOK

The text in your hands seeks to do more than merely aid Christian leaders of midsize congregations to embrace the realities that accompany churches of medium-size. Its primary purpose is to advance the actual accomplishment of faithful and fruitful work in that context. The goal of this resource is to equip you as a pastor or leader of a midsize church to increase the effectiveness of the mission and ministry carried out by your midsize congregation.

As will be demonstrated in the next chapter, approximately one-fourth of all congregations in the United States fall into the category of being medium-sized, numbering over seventy-five thousand churches. Yet little has been written to champion or support this specific size culture among churches. There are many megachurch conferences for equipping large congregations (and wanna-be large churches). Most of the classical pastoral approaches promoted in seminaries have served the smaller churches well. But medium-size churches, comprising nearly one in four congregations and serving twenty-five percent of the church-affiliated population (over forty million people), are left to find their way through the morass of mission and ministry without a roadmap. A glaring lacuna exists regarding resources designed specifically for the midsize church. Granted, there are up-to-date books, manuals, and online resources that provide some assistance to midsize churches. I am indebted to these in the development of this book, as will become clear as you read it. But what they lack—and here is the lacuna—is a singular and comprehensive focus on the distinctive dynamics of medium congregations.

Leading the midsize church in a manner that best advances the purposes entrusted to it by God doesn't happen automatically. It requires insight, intentionality, and effort. Accordingly, leadership in a medium church may feel like the right fit for you; it may be just right. But don't expect it to be facile if you are being faithful. You are called to lead this midsize ministry to achieve its most positive potential. That is a challenge. You will need help. And that is the purpose of this book. It will aid you in advancing the mission of your church and accomplishing the purposes that God has entrusted to it.

TO THE MAX

The title of this book expresses its intended outcome—that you are equipped to *maximize* the mission and ministry efforts of the midsize church you serve. Some may read the word *maximize* and assume it means to make larger. In some contexts that is an appropriate application of the term, since dictionaries typically offer the word *enlarge* as an option for its definition. In such a case this book might help you to enlarge the membership of your church so that it grows into a large congregation.

Capitalize for the sake of the Gospel

But that is not the primary purpose of this book. Instead, a different meaning of the word *maximize* is intended. It can also mean to make the most of something. In other words, this book seeks to help you to lead a midsize church to achieve the highest level of effectiveness possible given its distinctive culture and dynamics. It guides you to celebrate the unique characteristics of a medium church and to capitalize on those characteristics for the sake of the gospel. It undertakes to help your church reach its fullest potential.

THE VALUE OF CONGREGATIONAL SIZE CATEGORIES

Congregations that manifest similar cultural traits can be organized into fixed categories. Some similarities are due to ethnic background or denominational heritage. Certainly a formative influence is theology; congregations that share a common theological confession will frequently display similar worldviews and practices. Commonalities may also derive from demographic factors such as the average age, educational level, and income of the members. Environmental factors such as community context (e.g., urban, rural) and regional values play important roles.

Generally speaking, however, a most significant variable that impacts cultural commonalities among congregations is size. Congregational analyst Lyle Schaller claimed that culture and size are the two most effective frames of reference for identifying broad congregational differences.[4] Gary McIntosh, another church analyst who has studied thousands of congregations, maintains the following: "There are numerous ways to define different types of churches. For example, various categories often used are theological position, ethnic heritage, rural-urban orientation, growth or decline, health, worship style, and the age of the congregation. However, the most useful system is to group churches by size. Comparing churches by size reveals more helpful information for faithful ministry than looking at their denomination, location, or any of the other numerous methods of comparison."[5]

The various distinctions which McIntosh identifies are not insignificant, especially when it comes to theological confession. Yet categorizing congregations according to size is useful because similarly sized churches share similar characteristics relating to organizational dynamics, leadership expectations, management needs, communication challenges, relationship style, and the necessity of planning.

RIGHT SIZING

Understanding the differences of congregational dynamics based on size distinctions offers benefits for healthy and productive leadership by pastors

---

4.   Lyle Schaller, *The Very Large Church: New Rules for Leaders* (Nashville: Abingdon, 2000), 27.
5.   Gary McIntosh, *One Size Doesn't Fit All* (Grand Rapids: Fleming H. Revell, 2006), 19.

and lay people. As will be demonstrated in the next chapter, congregations fall into three broad cultural categories that reflect differing sizes: small, medium, and large. Each of these categories or types has distinctive characteristics regarding organization, programming, planning, and communication. Recognizing these distinctions in size typology will help you as a pastor or lay leader to understand why members of a church behave the way they do. Such insight will enable you to communicate appropriately and effectively. It guides you to avoid pitfalls and better to deal with problems and conflict when such arise.

Gary McIntosh describes this as *right sizing* the efforts of a congregation and its leadership, as follows: "Churches operate differently depending on the size of the congregation. 'Right sizing' the various ministries and processes of communicating, welcoming, training, involving, and a host of other activities is crucial for smooth operation, as well as increased growth, of a church. As a church grows, it cannot simply employ business-as-usual practices. Larger churches are not just bigger versions of smaller churches; in reality they are an entirely different entity that requires different operational procedures."[6]

In other words, small churches of less than 150 in average weekly worship attendance share a similar personality type, that is, cultural characteristics that are distinctive to their size. Large churches of 400 or more worshippers share distinguishing characteristics that unite them into a culture category. Most germane to the focus of this book is that midsize congregations (150 to 400 worshippers) demonstrate commonalities unique to their size. Wise leaders will recognize and appreciate the differences between the size categories. Aware of these distinctions, they will capitalize on the strengths and opportunities characteristic of the size of the congregations that they lead and serve.

Viewing this from another perspective, the failure to recognize the commonalities within size categories and the disparities between such categories can lead to unnecessary misfires in ministry. A large church is not simply a bigger manifestation of a small church, so one should not import practices that work in a large church to a small one and expect the same results. Nor is a small church merely a condensed version of a midsize church. The organizational and relational dynamics are more complex than that! Timothy Keller observes thus:

> One of the most common reasons for pastoral leadership mistakes is blindness to the significance of church size. Size has an enormous impact on how a church functions. There is a "size culture" that profoundly affects how decisions are made, how relationships flow, how effectiveness is evaluated, and what ministers, staff, and lay leaders do.

---

6. Gary McIntosh, *Taking Your Church to the Next Level* (Grand Rapids: Baker Books, 2009), 116.

We tend to think of the chief differences between churches mainly in denominational or theological terms, but that underestimates the impact of size on how a church operates. The difference between how churches of 100 and 1000 function may be much greater than the difference between a Presbyterian and a Baptist church of the same size. The staff person who goes from a church of 400 to a church of 2,000 is in many ways making a far greater change than if he or she moved from one denomination to another.

Behavior
& Mind Set

A large church is not simply a bigger version of a small church. The difference in communication, community formation, and decision-making processes are so great that the leadership skills required in each are of almost completely different orders.[7]

It is for this reason that congregation leaders must literally size up the situation in which they find themselves. They do this by recognizing that differently sized congregations will display differing cultural patterns while churches of similar size will share many characteristics of a common culture. There are predictable ways of being a church that cohere with different size gradients. By aligning to those predictable modes, pastors and church leaders will maximize mission and ministry efforts. They can right size those efforts for greatest effectiveness and productivity.

MAKING THE MOST OF YOUR CALLING
(AND THAT OF YOUR CHURCH)

This right sizing of your efforts as a leader of a medium church is the purpose of this book. It is a resource for pastors and leaders of midsize congregations—churches with an average weekend worship attendance in the range of 150 to 400 people. Its goal is not necessarily to facilitate the growth of a church from midsize to large. If God grants that numeric growth, to him be the glory! But a Christian assembly can faithfully carry out the calling that God gives to it within this size category without eventually transitioning to a larger size. You can be content with the size of your church, but you should never be complacent about its condition. God may not be calling your church to grow large at this time. But he does call you to cultivate its health. He calls you to develop its strengths. He wills for you to maximize its opportunities for mission and for ministry. This book is a resource for you to respond affirmatively to God's call for healthy and fruitful leadership of the midsize church.

---

7.   Keller, *Leadership and Church Size Dynamics*, 1.

CHAPTER 2

PERSPECTIVE

The Elders Board at Faith Church had a standing policy that members of the church could attend any regularly scheduled meeting to express concerns about the congregation. Gordon was tired of being the sole lightning rod for Emily's complaints about developments in the church, so he invited her to attend the next meeting of the Board of Elders in order to voice her complaints to others.

After the opening devotional reading presented by Pastor Burke, Gordon introduced Emily to the members of the board, "Most of us know Emily Hart. She is a founding member of this church. She has some concerns about the direction in which the church is going, so I invited her to bring them to our Elders Board. So Emily, go ahead and tell us what is on your mind."

Although Emily was thin and diminutive, she donned a forceful personality. She confidently addressed the seven members of the board, "I am here because I have fears about the direction in which this church is going. We are getting too large and impersonal! Almost fifty years ago my husband and I joined the effort to start this church because we wished to be part of a small and tight community.

"In those beginning years, our church was like a family. It was wonderful! It was true that we grew, but we were still a small church. In fact, until about fifteen years ago, Faith Church retained that feeling of being a close-knit family. But that's not my church anymore! That's not *this* church anymore! Now we are a *large* church! But I'm not going to leave it after being here so long. I have too many close friends and connections here. Many people still are like family to me here. But most are not. And it is all because we've become a *big* church!"

At this point Jack interrupted. Jack was the newer member of the Board of Elders who advocated for a vision quite divergent from Emily's. "Pardon me, Mrs. Hart," Jack interjected. "But what you are saying *astounds* me! Are you actually claiming that Faith Church is a *large* church? Are you saying that it is not a *small* church? Why, this is the smallest church that I have ever been a part of! This is definitely a *little* church, and if it got any smaller I don't think it would survive. We're lucky if we get over 250 in worship on any given Sunday—that's only a bit over one hundred in each service. Why, when I come to church it feels downright *tiny* to me.

"The fact is," Jack continued, "If we remain small and don't grow we will go the way of Ma and Pa grocery stores of the past. I remember one as a kid. It was a quaint little store located on a corner in my neighborhood. I liked to go there to buy candy and soda. But it is no longer in existence, not with the Walmarts and big supermarkets that have arisen. And that is what will happen to this little church unless we start doing things differently. We need to begin behaving like a larger church rather than a small one. Otherwise Faith Church will get smaller, as you desire, but it will not survive!"

A MATTER OF PERSPECTIVE

The dialog between Emily and Jack shows the difference that *perspective* makes. What a difference of opinion exists between the veteran member and the new kid on the block! Emily viewed Faith Church as a *large* congregation. From her perspective the church was big. Jack took a contrary view. In his perspective, Faith Church was *small*.

Placing a congregation into a size category is a matter of perspective. Whose categorization of Faith Church is accurate? Was Emily correct to identify the congregation as large? Or was Jack on target to label it a small church? In order for there to be consensus on this matter, a common perspective of the church's size would need to be reached.

This chapter provides *perspective* to the issue of church size. It will deliver a methodology for categorizing congregations by size. This is done by defining the boundaries for those categories through criteria that are anything but arbitrary. It will establish distinctions between small, midsize, and large churches that are demonstrable and discrete. This chapter also gives perspective regarding the scope and significance of middle-size congregations relative to other sizes of congregations. This will be done by comparing it to the proportion of small and large churches in America as well as to the percentages of worshippers attending each size category.

From the perspective offered in this book, both Emily and Jack are incorrect. Faith Church isn't a large church, as Emily purports. Neither is it a small congregation, as Jack maintains. It is a *medium* church!

DEFINING SIZE CATEGORIES

At this point you probably are wondering what specifically is meant when referring to a midsize church. How is it defined? What are the parameters that differentiate the midsize congregation from the small church and the large one? As will be seen, there is no absolute consensus among those who have studied congregational size on those parameters, although there is emerging agreement.

There is consensus in the metrics, however, the means for measuring size. Almost all sources identify the *average weekend worship attendance* as providing the best numeric indicator for categorizing congregations into various sizes.[1] Measuring average worship attendance is better than measuring congregational membership because it is a more accurate barometer of the active participation in the church. Moreover, it is a more consistent metric in comparing congregations where the variables of demographics, definition of membership, and denominational idiosyncrasies make problematic the use of membership numbers.[2] For example, some membership rosters do not include children while others do. Definitions vary regarding at what age adult membership begins. Many congregations retain a significant number of inactive members on their membership rolls, while others do not. Finally, categories of membership differ from denomination to denomination. These factors render the use of membership as an inaccurate and inconsistent metric for comparing congregations and for categorizing them into size divisions.

Although there is little disagreement regarding the use of average weekend attendance as the metric for categorizing churches into sizes, there is divergence regarding what the parameters of those categories should be. Several decades ago Lyle Schaller categorized congregations into seven classes: fellowship (less than 35 average worshippers), small (35–100), middle-size (100–175), awkward size (175–225), large (225–450), huge (450–700), and mini-denomination (700 or more).[3] Schaller's trilogy of books on church sizes, however, indicates that he operated with three major divisions: small (less than 100), middle-size (100–199), and large (more than 200).[4]

Although the three basic categories—small, medium, and large—have been employed by many observers of congregational life, they have not used the same numeric boundaries. Typically those boundaries have been adjusted upwardly from Schaller's initial designations. For example, Gary McIntosh differentiates between church sizes using the formula of small (15–200), medium (201–400), and large (401+).[5]

Another system of categorization worth considering is that developed by researchers affiliated with the Alban Institute. This schema originated with Arlin Rothauge who divided congregations into four classes: the family church (0–50), the pastoral church (50–150), the program church

---

1. Average weekend worship attendance is calculated by adding the number of worshippers of all ages present during weekend worship services (typically Sunday morning and Saturday evening, but potentially including other configurations such as Thursday evening or Monday night) during one year and then dividing that total by fifty-two.

2. Mark Chaves, *Congregations in America* (Cambridge, MA: Harvard University Press, 2004), 17.

3. Lyle Schaller, *The Multiple Staff and the Larger Church* (Nashville: Abingdon, 1980), 28.

4. Lyle Schaller, *The Middle Sized Church: Problems and Prescriptions* (Nashville: Abingdon, 1985), 7.

5. McIntosh, *One Size Doesn't Fit All,* 18.

(150–350), and the corporation church (350–500+).[6] This typology has been widely accepted as an accurate means of defining different types of congregations based on their size. The genius of Rothauge's schema is that it identifies four distinct congregational cultures, and the dynamics inherent to each culture have far-reaching implications. This typology has served as the basis for analyzing church cultures by subsequent writers affiliated with the Alban Institute.[7] Most notable among these is Alice Mann, whose research will be considered shortly.

IDENTIFYING THE BOUNDARIES

It is widely acknowledged that Christian congregations have a systemic quality. In other words, a church is a social system, and the systems operate most efficiently within certain size parameters. "Each system has elements which bring energy, life, and growth," observes Kevin Martin, "The system also has elements that keep the system from becoming too large. In systems theory, elements that bring energy to a system are called 'reinforcers,' whereas those that contain energy are called 'balancers.' These two types of elements keep the system within certain boundaries. . . . In other words, each system has a reinforcing style that is characteristic of that size and that produces a congregational culture."[8] Research indicates that the system commonly referred to as the midsize church has boundaries that are marked at the lower end with the numeric factor of 150 and at the upper end at the number 400. This aligns closely with Rothauge's category of the program size church, which he identified as being bound by the lower limit of 150 worshippers and the upper limit of 350 worshippers. Let's take a closer look at these lower and upper numeric boundaries.

There is remarkable agreement that the number 150 for average worship attendance is a significant transition point in the size makeup of a religious congregation like a church.[9] British anthropologist Robin Dunbar investigated the social groupings of tribal peoples and discovered that the average size of a tribal group was around 148 members.[10] This resulted in a formula known as the Rule of 150. According to this rule, when a social organization reaches a size of 150 people, the complexity

6. Arlin Routhage, *Sizing Up a Congregation for New Member Ministry* (New York: Seabury, 1983), 5.
7. Beth Ann Gaede, ed., *Size Transitions in Congregations* (Herndon, VA: Alban Institute, 2001). This book provides a compendium of essays composed by over a dozen writers who build on Rothauge's taxonomy.
8. Kevin Martin, *The Myth of the 200 Level* (Nashville: Abingdon, 2005), 32.
9. Kevin Martin reports that even Lyle Schaller revised his definition of a small church so that the upper limit no longer was 100 but 150 average worshippers. This means that Schaller recalibrated the lower limit for medium churches to 150. See Martin, *The Myth of the 200 Barrier*, 11.
10. Robin Dunbar, "Coevolution or NeoCortical Size, Group Size and Language in Humans," *Behavior and Brain Sciences* 16, no. 4 (1993): 681–702.

of interrelationships between the people results either in a division of the group or the dissolution of the group altogether. Similarly the number 150 marks a significant paradigm shift for the organizational design and structure of a congregation. "At about 150," Alice Mann observes, "a qualitative shift (the 'tipping point') occurs and a true organization comes into being with official roles and structures, formal communication, and explicit procedures."[11] This is why at this size churches become more programmatic in nature, which explains Rothauge's designation of such congregations as *program size*.

Routhauge originally set the upper boundary of the program church at 350 average worship attenders. However, he later became convinced that this number was too low.[12] Alice Mann has revised the limit upward to 400.[13] Similarly, Gary McIntosh has consistently recognized 400 as the maximum attendance for the medium-sized church.[14] The reason behind this identification of a terminus is the existence of a sociological ceiling. The numeric range of 350 to 400 average worshippers marks a transition to a new and distinct system of organization. Above that transition the congregation operates more like a corporation, as Routhage observed, with increased complexity and diversity involving multiple sub-congregations. In most cases an average worship attendance of 400 functions as a ceiling to the midsize church and a floor to the large church.

FLOORS AND CEILINGS

The above-cited research analysis supports the numeric figures for a lower boundary for the mid-size church at 150 average worshippers and an upper boundary at 400 worshippers. This is because there are demonstrable plateau levels for congregational sizes. Evidence demonstrates that congregations cluster within definite and predictable size ranges.[15] The transition zones between these ranges are frequently referred to as plateau levels or even glass ceilings because of the extraordinary effort that is takes to transition in size beyond those zones.

Using Rothauge's framework, Alice Mann identifies three critical plateau zones that separate four categories of congregational sizes. These zones are illustrated in the following graphic (numerals identify average weekend attendance):[16]

---

11. Alice Mann, *Raising the Roof: The Pastoral-to-Program Size Transition* (Herndon, VA: Alban Institute, 2001), 5.

12. Gaede, *Size Transitions in Congregations*, 27.

13. Mann, *Raising the Roof*, 7.

14. McIntosh, *One Size Doesn't Fit All*, 18; *Taking Your Church to the Next Level*, 145.

15. Alice Mann, *The In-Between Church: Navigating Size Transitions in Congregations* (Herndon, VA: Alban Institute, 1998), 11–15; McIntosh, *Taking Your Church to the Next Level*, 129–32;

16. The chart provides information from two worksheets provided on pages 17–18 of Mann, *The In-Between Church*.

Corporate Size (400+)
Plateau Zone (350–400)
Program Size (200–350)
Plateau Zone (150–200)
Pastoral Size (70–150)
Plateau Zone (50–70)
Family Size (2–50)

As previously stated, the transition zones between the conventional ranges in size are often identified as plateau levels or glass ceilings. The metaphorical language helps one envision the issues involved. The concept of a *plateau* presents the image of the floor upon which one walks. The image of a *ceiling* depicts the upper barrier to habitable space.

Applied to church sizes these transition zones function similar to horizontal structural barriers in a multi-story building. Consider the illustration of a three-story house. People are able to inhabit each of the three stories of this house. They can comfortably live and move within those stories, and indeed they spend the vast majority of their time residing within the space of each story. Although they are able to move from one level of the home to another, they don't normally live in the transition zones, which are the stairways. Moreover, the passage from one level to the other is only possible through the stairways. One doesn't regularly burrow through the ceiling of one story to enter into the next level.

Now consider this same image as it relates to church sizes:

LARGE CHURCH
350–400 Plateau
MEDIUM CHURCH
150–200 Plateau
SMALL CHURCH

Because of various relational, sociological, cultural, and systemic dynamics, church members will comfortably inhabit the living spaces of the small church, mid-size church, and large church.[17] Alice Mann refers to this inhab-

---

17. For the purposes of this analysis three categories of church size are used rather than Rothauge's four categories. The family-size and pastoral-size categories are integrated into one depicted as the small church. This does not reject the value of distinguishing between the two categories, however. Similarly, Susan Beaumont has identified three distinct categories of the large church: professional (400–800 average worshippers), strategic (800–1200 worshippers), and matrix

itable domain as *sociological space.*[18] But people do not reside comfortably within the plateau zones. In fact, these zones provide a structural function. The 150–200 plateau operates as a ceiling for the small church, effectively acting as an upper numeric barrier to the living space for the members of a small size church. But this same 150–200 plateau functions as a floor to the midsize church, providing support to its inhabitable social space. Likewise, the 350–400 plateau serves to hinder transition from the medium to the large sized church, but offers support to the systemic stability of the large church.

The point of this illustration is that there exist demonstrable systemic and cultural divisions in churches based on the size of the church. These divisions or groupings are not arbitrarily identified, but they are determined by the social and organizational dynamics that are inherent to each size system.

In light of these observations, the boundaries of the midsize church used in this book are 150 minimum and 400 maximum average weekend worshippers. Accordingly, we will operate with this definition of the midsize church.[19]

SLICING THE PIE: PROPORTION OF CONGREGATIONS

Having defined the midsize church by its numeric parameters, the question now arises regarding the prevalence of middle-sized churches in America. How many congregations in America fall into this category? If all the churches in the United States are depicted in a pie graph, what proportion of the pie is comprised by the category labeled *midsize church*?

Estimates vary slightly regarding this question. In 1998 the National Congregations Study (NCS) surveyed clergy, staff, and lay leaders of 1,236 Congregations in the United States.[20] This research indicated that over twenty percent of congregations fall into the category of the midsize church.[21]

(1200+ worshippers). The designation of a singular large church, as presented in this book, does not reject these more refined distinctions. See Susan Beaumont, *Inside the Large Congregation* (Herndon, VA: Alban Institute, 2011), 43–60.

18. Mann, *Raising the Roof*, 10.

19. These numeric borders are zones, not precise transitional points. Within these zones congregations will demonstrate characteristics from both sides of the transition. For example, a congregation with the average worship attendance of 165 may reflect some attributes that are typical of a small church as well as other attributes characteristic of a midsize church. Similarly, a congregation with an average worship attendance of 385 may already demonstrate significant resemblance to a large church, although by these metrics it is still classified as a middle-sized church. In addition, these boundaries apply to what one might call an ordinary midsize church. However, there are exceptions to the rule. The dynamics involved in these exceptions are described and analyzed by Theodore Johnson in Gaede, *Size Transitions in Congregations*, 13–15, 28.

20. Chaves, *Congregations in America*, 217–18.

21. Chaves, *Congregations in America*, 19. The figure of twenty percent applies specifically to congregations which have an average of 140 to 350 "regularly participating individuals." Precise figures for the boundaries of 150 to 400 are not provided in the NCS report.

A second source of data is the Faith Community Today (FACT) survey that studied congregations in America. This survey, conducted in 2010 by the Hartford Institute for Religion Research, involved over eleven thousand randomly sampled congregations. According to this research, a solid twenty-five percent—one quarter—of the congregations surveyed reported a median weekend worship attendance of 150 to 400. By way of comparison, small congregations—those averaging fewer than 150 worshippers—amount to fifty-nine percent of all congregations. And large congregations with over 400 average worshippers comprise about sixteen percent.[22] This means that there are almost four times as many small congregations as large ones in the United States.

In light of these data, one can confidently assert that midsize churches comprise between one-fifth (twenty percent) and one-fourth (twenty-five percent) of the congregations in the United States. As a portion of the pie, this percentage would appear like this as compared to the other two sizes of congregations, using the findings from the FACT survey:

Congregations in the United States

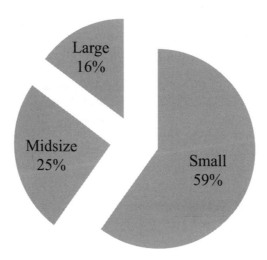

This pie graph illustrates that by far the largest proportion of congregations—six out of ten—are small, averaging less than 150 in weekend worship attendance. On the other hand, large churches make up a very small fraction of the total number of churches—about sixteen percent.

22. "2010 National Survey of Congregations," *Faith Communities Today 2010 National Survey of Congregations: Frequencies for the Entire Survey Population* (Hartford, CT: Hartford Institute for Religion Research, 2011), 9, accessed November 1, 2017, http://faithcommunitiestoday.org/sites/default/files/2010FrequenciesV1.pdf.

Midsize congregations comprise a quarter of all U.S. congregations, unquestionably a significant segment of religious assemblies in America.

SLICING THE PIE: PROPORTION OF WORSHIPPERS

But this is only part of the story. The National Congregations Study indicates that a disproportionately high number of worshippers attend large churches—roughly half of all churchgoers.[23] In other words, fifty percent of worshippers gather in about fifteen percent of churches, those with an average attendance of 400 plus. Approximately twenty-five percent of worshippers will be found in a midsize church with an average worship attendance of 150 to 400.[24] And another twenty-five percent are found in small churches, averaging less than 150 in worship. Put another way, most congregations are small (approximately sixty percent), but as many people worship in large congregations as in small and midsize churches combined (fifty percent). Thus the pie can be sliced in this manner:

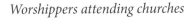
Worshippers attending churches

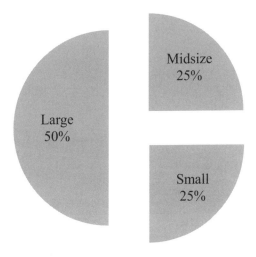

The bottom line for midsize churches is that in regard to all congregations and worshippers in the United States, they subsume about a quarter of

---

23.   Chaves, *Congregations in America*, 18–19.

24.   Chaves, *Congregations in America*, 19. The NCS reports a figure of twenty percent, which applies specifically to congregations that have an average of 180–400 "regularly participating individuals." Another ten percent applies to congregations consisting of 125–180 participants. When this latter percentage is divided to align more closely with the 150–180 participant number—i.e., five percent—and this figure is added to the original twenty percent, the total approximates twenty-five percent. Precise figures for the boundaries of 150–400 are not provided in the NCS report.

congregations and a quarter of worshippers. But this does not make these congregations insignificant. In 2014 a Gallup Poll indicated that forty-one percent of Americans claim to attend worship services regularly (weekly or almost weekly) and fifty-three percent report attending religious services at least monthly.[25] Since the population of the United States is about 320 million, this means that upwards of 170 million Americans claim to attend worship services at least monthly. One-fourth of this number equates to over forty-two million worshippers in midsize congregations. In other words, it is possible that upwards of forty million people are associated with middle-size congregations in the United States. Taken from another perspective, there are over 300,000 congregations in the United States.[26] Of this number approximately 75,000—twenty-five percent—are of medium-size.

Wouldn't it be great to mobilize these 75,000 congregations to achieve their maximum capacity for effectiveness? Wouldn't it be a game changer if the forty-plus million churchgoers who attend midsize churches would be better equipped and empowered for engaging in God's ministry and advancing his mission? There is great potential in the midsize church! This book seeks to maximize that potential.

MULTIPLE POINTS OF PERSPECTIVE

This chapter has been about perspective. Its purpose is to establish a shared vantage point from which the middle-sized church can be viewed. But the best perspective of an object is achieved through multiple vantage points.

Take your eyesight as an example. If you close one eye your perspective changes. You lose some depth perception. Your vision becomes two dimensional rather than seeing things in three dimensions. This is the reason why people who have lost sight in one eye oftentimes are denied permission to drive a vehicle. They lack the ability to perceive distances between objects, such as how close or how far ahead another car is. But with two eyes—two portals for perspective—the mind is able to comprehend depth and estimate distances accurately. Multiple sources of sight provide a different and better perspective.

Another example of this dynamic is found in the use of surveillance cameras. Companies that install security systems using video surveillance strongly recommend against using a sole camera. The reason is not just that the agency wishes to sell more cameras to make a larger profit. The primary purpose of positioning cameras in multiple locations is to provide more thorough surveillance—one could say *perspective*—of the area being watched.

---

25. Frank Newport, "Three-Quarters of Americans Identify as Christian," Gallup News, December 24, 2014, accessed November 1, 2017, http://www.gallup.com/poll/180347/three-quarters-americans-identify-christian.aspx?utm_source=RELIGION_AND_SOCIAL_TRENDS&utm_medium=topic&utm_campaign=tiles.
26. Chaves, *Congregations in America*, 3.

The effort to achieve an accurate and comprehensive perspective of the midsize church will employ multiple vantage points. One such position for analysis is internal—looking at the midsize church from within. But other vantage points are external, specifically from the positions of the other two main categories of congregations—small and large churches. Consequently, in subsequent chapters the medium church will be examined by comparing it to the typical small congregation and to the typical large one. The reason for this is because the midsize church possesses characteristics of both the small church and large church.[27] By considering the middle-sized church from these two perspectives, a more accurate understanding of the distinctive dynamics of this category of church will emerge.

SUMMARY

This chapter has provided increased clarity regarding the object of study in this book—the midsize church. We have adjusted the lens of investigation so that our focus becomes more defined. The metric for identifying a congregation's size is its average weekend worship attendance. This determines whether it is categorized as a small church, medium church, or large church. The boundaries for the middle-size church are 150 average worshippers as a minimum and 400 worshippers as the upper limit. Although in reality these are not hard boundaries, they serve as useful parameters for categorizing churches into size types. The size distinctions between small, midsize, and large churches are not arbitrarily chosen. Observable sociological and organizational differences exist among the three categories.

This chapter also has provided perspective on the significance of midsize churches in America relative to the other categories (small and large). Medium-sized congregations comprise approximately one out of four churches in the United States and involve an equal proportion (twenty-five percent) of America's worshippers. This is a significant percentage of Christians who can mobilize for mission to the world and ministry toward one another. But in order to maximize such mobilization, leaders of midsize churches need to understand some of the challenges and opportunities that are distinctive to this size culture. That will be the focus of study for the next two chapters.

---

27. McIntosh, *One Size Doesn't Fit All*, 31–34. McIntosh maintains that the medium-size church manifests transitional characteristics between the small congregation and large one.

CHAPTER 3

PERILS

Pastor Andrew Burke and his wife, Brenda, were sharing pillow talk before retiring to sleep. They discussed the new normal in their household—life with a teenager. Their oldest child, a son named Jonathan, had turned thirteen only eight months earlier. He, his siblings, and his parents were adjusting to the changes that the teen years bring.

"Adolescence is such an awkward and perilous age!" exclaimed Brenda. "A teenager lives midway between childhood and adulthood. I see it in Jonathan. On the one hand, he wants me to love him. But on the other hand he doesn't want his friends to see me with him. He insists on being independent and on making his own decisions. Yet oftentimes he acts about as responsibly—or I should say, irresponsibly—as he did when he was nine years old. He tries to act grown up, but I still recognize in him characteristics of a little boy. And then there are the wild emotions I see in him! He's definitely not as emotionally stable as before. I can see why many teenagers are at risk. It's a perilous age! It's just all very awkward!"

"I remember being thirteen," reflected Andrew. "You are right—you have one foot in childhood and one precariously on the stairway to becoming an adult. I recall the excitement of new freedoms and opportunities to venture on my own, but there were many landmines and perils along that path. I was eager and fearful at the same time. I guess the one thing that can be said about adolescence is that it is full of potential. On the one hand, there is potential for growth, maturity, and making one's mark on the world for good. On the other hand, there are so many possibilities to make bad decisions. There are feelings of accomplishment, but also the sense of inadequacy and the experience of low esteem. Let's take some time now, Brenda, to pray for Jonathan. More than ever before, he needs to know that God is present with him and loves him through this awkward period of life."

The next day Brenda reflected on this discussion about their son. She thought about how challenging life had become for her firstborn. But then her thoughts turned to the congregation that her husband pastored. "I've oftentimes used that same word—*awkward*—to describe our church," she mused. "In some ways, it is like a teenager."

Brenda began to draw comparisons. "A teen is midway between a child and an adult, displaying characteristics of each. So our congregation is midway between a small church and a large one. Sometimes it acts like a small church, at other times it seems more like a big church." She thought of another comparison: "Just like Jonathan sometimes wants affection from me and sometimes wants distance, I find members of Faith Church to have a similar ambivalence. Many of the people desire direct delivery of pastoral care to them, like a child wanting a parent to attend to his every need. But then at other times they act as if they want distance from the pastor—for my husband to be more 'hands off' in the efforts of the church."

Brenda considered other similarities between her teenage son and her church. Faith Church seemed more vulnerable than some other churches she had been involved with. Sometimes she perceived a sense of low corporate self-esteem, not unlike the poor self-image that some teenagers reflect. Yet she had never been at a church that had more potential for productivity and impact for the kingdom of God. Faith Church held much promise to "come into its own" and make a difference in the lives of its members and community.

Brenda recognized that Faith Church, this intermediate sized congregation, held much potential to flourish, but also to flounder. In some ways it was at risk. In other ways it showed promise to truly come into its own. Everything just seemed so awkward! The church was very much like her teenage son—so full of potential, both for peril and for promise!

POTENTIAL POSSIBILITIES

The word *potential* can be used to convey both good news and bad news. It usually is associated with the positive. When an employer describes a worker as having potential, or an educator depicts a student as such, or a coach labels a player in this way, it typically is a favorable descriptor. It means this person has the qualities that can contribute to success.

But the word also can mean that this individual hasn't yet achieved what he is capable of. He hasn't yet reached his potential. Furthermore, it can infer problems, perils, and pitfalls. There is the possibility for danger, difficulty, and defeat. In this sense, the person is at risk of failing. He is at risk of faltering in his calling and purpose.

In the next two chapters we will consider what distinctive potentialities face the typical midsize church. In this chapter we will investigate the potential *perils* that many medium-sized congregations confront. These perils present challenges that must be recognized and proactively addressed. In the subsequent chapter we will analyze the potential opportunities that midsize churches may pursue in order to flourish. This is the midsize church's *promise* of advantages for advancing God's mission and ministry.

Each middle-sized parish has its unique challenges and difficulties. These vary from congregation to congregation. However, there are some common problems and perils that are shared by most midsize churches. In the next pages we will investigate four such threats to the viability and vitality of medium congregations. Leaders of this size parish should be aware of these typical pitfalls so that they can navigate around them successfully and guide the church to safe waters.

(1) AWKWARD IDENTITY *between Small + Large*

The first characteristic of most midsize congregations that presents a potential peril is their inherent awkwardness. In his book, *The Middle Sized Church: Problems and Prescriptions*, Lyle Schaller ascribed the label *the awkward-sized church* to medium congregations.[1] He maintained that the word *awkward* aptly describes the condition of most of these parishes. Similarly, Herb Miller asserts that this word—*awkward*—best summarizes the unique behavior dynamics of medium-sized churches.[2] The reason for this is because, like the awkward teenage years, midsize churches have characteristics that are transitional in nature. The adolescent demonstrates some attributes of childhood and some of adulthood, oftentimes clumsily combined.

The midsize congregation demonstrates characteristics both of the small church and of the large church, and it can be a challenge to navigate successfully between these two orientations. Gary McIntosh compares the midsize church to a stretched cell in a living organism—in the transition between a single cell entity (the small church) and the multiple cell organism (the large church)—that may be an unstable condition.[3]

This instability has been noted by various congregational researchers. Lyle Schaller maintained that the middle-sized church is often a very vulnerable organization.[4] Such congregations typically are stretched for resources such as staff, programming, and systems for assimilation and retention of members. This instability means that an internal disruption can deliver a disproportionately detrimental impact upon the health of the church. Herb Miller observes that some families will bypass midsize churches in preference for larger churches that provide more varied and polished worship services, preaching, and programs. He maintains that medium churches can appropriately be referred to as being a *dangerous size* as well as an awkward one.[5]

---

1. Schaller, *The Middle Sized Church*, 99.
2. Herb Miller, *Church Effectiveness Nuggets, Volume 18: Navigating toward Maximum Effectiveness in Midsize Churches* (N.p.: Herb Miller, 2009), 10.
3. McIntosh, *One Size Doesn't Fit All*, 43–45.
4. Schaller, *The Middle Sized Church*, 103.
5. Miller, *Navigating toward Maximum Effectiveness in Midsize Churches*, 17.

② CONFLICTING EXPECTATIONS

A second dynamic typical of medium-sized parishes is that frequently competing agendas and expectations exist among members. A parent of a teenager understands the challenge of holding appropriate expectations for an adolescent daughter or son. On the one hand, the parent may wish for the teen to continue to behave like a younger child by being affectionate to mom and open to dad's direction. On the other hand, the parent will expect the adolescent to be more responsible in carrying out duties and more independent in making decisions. Not only is it awkward for the young person, it is awkward for the parent to know what to expect! So also midsize congregations are oftentimes caught in the tension of people's expectations, some of which contradict each another.

The differing expectations for Faith Church that were depicted earlier between Emily, the founding member, and Jack, the new member, illustrate this tension. Emily desired characteristics of Faith Church that were more in line with a small congregation, especially regarding pastoral care needs. Jack advocated for attributes that typify a large church with its proliferation of polished programming. Each had expectations for this medium-sized church that were in conflict with the other.

The conflicting expectations between those who promote small church values and those who advocate large church culture are palpable. Indeed, some members want the best of both worlds. For example, members typically want the medium-sized church to provide the close relational feel of a small church. They expect it to be like the theme song from the *Cheers* television series where everybody knows your name. But these same people also want a church that offers a multiplicity of program options characteristic of large churches.

Kevin Martin identifies the midsize congregation as a *hybrid* church. It possesses elements that exist in both small churches (e.g., relatively few human and financial resources) and large churches (e.g., expanded program offerings). But this leads to expectations that are mixed as well. Martin observes that it is not only members and newcomers who express these mixed expectations to the leadership of the congregation. Frequently even pastors, professional staff, and lay leaders communicate the mixed message that can lead to confusion and ambiguity.[6]

Tangible tensions arise from these mixed expectations. On the one hand are those who pine for the characteristics of a small church. "People who prefer a smaller church environment issue calls for a return to a simpler church where everyone can know each other," Gary McIntosh writes. "This may take the form of a request to eliminate multiple worship services in favor of returning to one service. Or it may come as a stated hope for more personal visits from the pastor or even eliminating a staff

---

6. Martin, *The Myth of the 200 Barrier*, 66.

member in the guise of cutting costs. Whatever form it takes, there will be regular pressure to return the church to one that has the relational characteristics of churches with fewer than 200 worshippers."[7]

On the other hand, there are those who push for the characteristics of a large church, who "may request an increased variety and number of ministry options, perhaps arising from real needs people are facing in their personal lives. . . . The possibilities are endless, but the pressures mount as some worshipers desire the church to move on to become a larger church."[8]

Some members, like Emily, have expectations that the church will act and feel like a small church—intimate, familial, and personal to all. Others, like Jack, expect the church to act large, with many options for worship style, program participation, and satisfaction of specialized needs. The challenge in managing these competing expectations is not to be all things to all people, but to define the church's identity and mission clearly and to live consistently with that identity and mission.

3 NEGATIVE SELF-IMAGE

A third dynamic that has potential to become problematic in a midsize congregation is a low corporate self-image. This is related to the previous issue of conflicting expectations.

Usually an established small church is content to remain small. Unless it is a church plant or mission congregation, its members typically don't expect the membership to grow or the worship attendance to increase. Members are content with the status quo, as long as the clergy are able to attend to their spiritual needs. The expectation of some small churches is simply to survive. So as long as they are surviving, they are succeeding. The self-image of the typical small congregation is not grandiose, but it also harbors little guilt about its identity and capacity. "We do what we can," is the mantra of its members, "And that is okay."

At the other end of the size spectrum is the large church. Such a parish in the United States typically has a positive corporate self-image because it embodies the American value of bigger is better. Although many large congregations are also challenged with the reality of having fewer resources than can meet people's wants and expectations, still much gets done. Furthermore, when a significant incongruity with the congregation's mission or vision is identified and owned by the church leadership, they are likely to redirect resources to correct the problem.

However, the expectations of members of medium-sized churches oftentimes are not met. They will frequently become consumed with what is lacking in their congregation's efforts to provide ministry or to

---

7.   McIntosh, *Taking Your Church to the Next Level*, 148.
8.   Ibid., 149.

advance the mission. They focus on problems and liabilities rather than on successes and potentialities. This can lead to frustration and discouragement. It is not uncommon for pastors, staff, and lay leaders—not to mention other lay members—to minimize the strengths of the medium-size church and to greatly underestimate its potential for good.

No doubt the biggest contributor to this malaise is the tendency of parishioners to compare their church to others. A well-known adage asserts that comparisons are odious. Indeed, comparing oneself to another person can lead to odious thinking and behavior—from pride and presumption on the one hand to inferiority and despair on the other. Typically poor self-esteem results from the perception that one doesn't compare well with others.

The low self-image of a middle-sized parish can result from members comparing their church to a small congregation. This was the case with Emily depicted earlier. She viewed the small church as the ideal, and so Faith Church had fallen from its original righteousness and was less than its potential. Paradoxically, others make the comparison and end up perceiving the medium church to be in fact a small church, and for them this is a negative identification. They accordingly minimize its potential to accomplish great things. They have modest expectations for the church, with a concomitant low image of its significance and value.

Many midsize congregations are not growing numerically in membership or attendance. Whereas a small church most likely is accepting of this reality, leaders of the midsize church frequently feel pressure to grow in size. When this doesn't happen, they often assume that they have failed.

Most likely a midsize church's poor corporate self-identity arises from comparisons with large churches, both in the immediate locale and in the media. This manifests itself as the little brother syndrome. Just as a small sibling is led to believe he is inferior to his big brother, so also the middle-size church perceives itself to be inferior to bigger congregations. In American society today large churches, especially megachurches (averaging more than two thousand in worship), have a disproportionately high visibility in the community. The large church's celebrity clergy, impressive facilities, extensive programming, professional presentation of worship services, state of the art public relations, and well publicized promotions contribute to the perception among midsize parishes that they don't measure up to the importance and impact of the large church. This comparison results in an inferiority complex among members of the medium church.

Yet perception is not reality. The medium-sized church's self-assessment as ineffective and insubstantial is usually not accurate. Actually, the contribution to the expansion of the kingdom of God made by a midsize congregation is significant. Lyle Schaller affirmed this impact years ago:

> In the typical middle-sized congregation there is far more going in terms of ministry, outreach, and service than meets the casual eye. Much of what is

happening is visible to relatively few members. Nine-tenths of the members are totally unaware of the redemptive ministry that is part of choir rehearsal on Thursday evening. Ninety-nine percent are unaware of a particular visit by the pastor or a concerned layperson to a lonely member in a nursing home. The vast majority are not aware of the extent in which the dollars given for missions are utilized to expand the ministry of the universal church. Relatively few have ever looked in on the third- and fourth-grade Sunday school class. This lack of detailed firsthand knowledge about the scope of that congregation's ministry makes it easy for many members to believe "this is a small church and there's not much going on here."[9]

The challenge is for pastors and leaders of midsize congregations to help their members—and themselves—to perceive the eternally weighty impact that their efforts are achieving. The challenge is for both professionals and parishioners in these churches to perceive the great things that *God* is doing among them and through them to advance his mission.

(4) PRESSURES ON THE PASTOR

A fourth dynamic typical of the midsize congregation, which has potential to become problematic, is the demands on the pastor. Arlin Routhage's depiction of the small church (composed of less than 150 average worshippers) as the *pastoral church* is telling.[10] This size category is so labeled because almost all of the relationships and activities in the congregation involve the pastor. The pastor is the hub of the wheel that is the system of this small church. The pastor not only leads worship, but teaches most Bible studies and education classes and attends prayer groups or social gatherings. When a member has a personal need or crisis, the pastor is readily available to provide direct pastoral care. The pastor knows every member and can address them by name. There is a direct personal relationship between the shepherd and each member of the flock.

However, when the number of active worshiping members exceeds 150, the "Rule of 150" takes effect. It is challenging for any but the most gifted human being to be able to know in depth this many people and to provide them with consistent, immediate, and direct pastoral care. "If clergy have the idea firmly fixed in their head that they are ineffective as a pastor unless they can relate in a profound way with every member of the parish," Alice Mann asserts, "then 150 active members (plus perhaps an even larger number of inactive members) is about all one person can manage."[11] But the midsize church is larger than this, and the needs of its members are significantly more demanding on the pastor's time and

---

9.   Schaller, *The Middle Sized Church*, 89–90.
10. Routhage, *Sizing Up a Congregation for New Member Ministry*, 5.
11. Mann, *The In-Between Church*, 82.

attention. Clergy will be stressed in their efforts to provide consistent, immediate, and direct attention to every member's expectations.

Accordingly, the functioning of clergy in the midsize church must differ dramatically from that of the small church. The role of the pastor is still highly significant, even central, to the life of the congregation. But his focus of activity should be to manage the delivery of ministry rather than to directly deliver it all. The execution of ministry is not isolated to one individual—the pastor—but is delivered through a team of leaders (staff and lay).

This in itself is not problematic. But it becomes a problem when pastors see the delivery of the ministry as their exclusive right and responsibility. If clergy claim the need and vocation to provide direct pastoral care and extensive personal attention to every member and prospective member of the congregation at all times, the task will likely be too heavy. There are too many individuals to track and too many needs to address. Either the pastor will burn out from the stress of attempting to care for the needs of the people, or those needs will not be addressed, or both. Sometimes the problem is the minister's unwillingness to share the load with others. In other cases the problem is that although the church is too large to be served adequately by one pastor, its members believe they cannot afford more than one paid staff member. As a result, the clergy person is expected to function like a parson in a small church, although the demands of a much larger congregation press upon him. This places enormous stress on ministers and their families.

SUMMARY

The middle-sized church is filled with potential. It has potential for problems as well as potential to prevail in its mission. Leaders of this size parish benefit from being aware of the typical pitfalls, so that they can navigate around them successfully.

Several problems frequently afflict the medium congregation. It can function awkwardly as if in a state of arrested development between a small and large size. Its members may embrace a poor corporate self-image, living in a perpetual state of discontentment as they focus on limitations and shortcomings. Its leaders face varied expectations by members, expectations that are often unrealistic and even conflicting. Pastors especially feel the stress of these expectations, and find themselves pressed to provide consistent, immediate, and direct attention to every member's needs.

Yet there is also the potential to prosper. Middle-size churches typically are presented with many distinctive opportunities to engage in fruitful mission and to provide meaningful ministry. This is the promising future that medium parishes possess. Leaders of these congregations should recognize these unique opportunities that the context of the midsize church affords, so that they may optimize the potential for fruitful ministry. This is the *promise* inherent to the midsize church that is celebrated in the next chapter.

CHAPTER 4

PROMISE

Michelle Sanchez reflected on her position as an officer of Faith Church. She had served on the church council for two years. It had been a very challenging time for her and the other elected leaders. But it also was very gratifying. Michelle experienced great fulfillment in this role of leadership.

When she accepted the responsibility of serving as a congregational officer, Michelle certainly didn't need more work put on her plate. As a mother of two middle-schoolers, she was consumed with a plentitude of parenting tasks. As an executive in the finance department of the community bank, she attended to several supervisory and fiduciary responsibilities. In addition, she was involved in a couple of civic organizations that demanded time and attention. But when she was asked to put her name forward for election as a church officer, Michelle believed that God's hand was guiding her to serve.

What made this role of leadership most meaningful to her was the sense of significance that she connected to it. Not significance for herself—Michelle didn't need a boost of ego—but significance regarding the impact of the mission of Faith Church. Michelle was convinced that there was no more important work to be done than the Lord's work. This brought blessing to people in this life and in the life to come. The church's ministry transformed lives for the better here on earth, and brought the promise of a perfect life hereafter. Michelle felt honored to be a participant in that work!

What especially excited her was the fact that Faith Church seemed to have such promise for the future. It possessed much potential for good! Michelle's own life—and that of her family members—had been greatly enriched by active involvement in the church. Through the nurturing ministry of Faith Church, she had grown in her relationship with the living Christ. She had been formed in the virtues of faith, hope, and love. She witnessed the ways in which her husband and two children had been changed for the better. So she sought to commend this to others.

When Michelle moved to the community ten years earlier, she and her husband could have joined a small church or a large congregation. But they selected Faith Church, a medium-sized parish. For them this size was just right. Because it wasn't small, the church could offer multiple ministry offerings and opportunities for enrichment and involvement. Michelle felt that she and her husband could find the niches in which they might serve that would maximize their interests and gifts. She also valued the ways in which the congregation ministered to its neighborhood and community; outreach was important to her. Yet she and her family members were being spiritually fed and nurtured, causing them to grow in their identity as disciples of Jesus. Particularly meaningful was the diversity of members at Faith Church, something that she felt was lacking in smaller churches that she had visited while church shopping. There were people of different races, ethnicities, ages, and social standings who gathered to worship the one Lord at Faith Church.

Michelle also valued characteristics of the church that distinguished it from large congregations that she had visited. Despite the diversity at Faith Church, there was a real sense of unity and wholeness. This holistic quality seemed to be intrinsic to the congregational culture. There also was a higher level of intimacy among members of the church, and ownership of its ministry by most, as compared to the more distant and detached connections she observed in larger congregations. Faith Church was large enough for diverse opportunities to be involved, yet small enough for close relationships with many members of the church.

Michelle was glad to have this opportunity to lead by serving, because she was convinced of the benefits that Faith Church was bringing to her family and to her community. She was convinced that this midsize congregation had great *promise* for making a positive difference in the lives of many!

THE POSITIVE PROSPECT OF PROMISE

The word *promise* usually has positive connotations. When we say that a situation is promising, this is an occasion for hope. When persons are described as holding promise, we expect great things of them. Even (especially!) in the Bible, the word promise is laden with grace and hope. So when this word, promise, is applied to a church, it is a favorable descriptor. It means the assembly has qualities that can lead to flourishing and blessing.

Accordingly, *promise* can be aptly applied to the medium church. In this chapter we will consider what distinctive positive potentialities portend for the typical midsize church. We will analyze the potential advantages that midsize churches may pursue in order to flourish. These potentialities provide opportunities unique to the midsize church to carry out effectively the mission and ministry that God has entrusted to it.

Having reflected upon potential perils that oftentimes plague midsize parishes, we will now investigate some inherent possibilities that contribute to the church's potential to flourish. There are characteristics distinctive to the size culture of a medium congregation that uniquely provide opportunities for it to carry out the mission and ministry that God has entrusted to it. This is how the midsize church demonstrates great *promise* for flourishing in its mission and ministry.

Just as every middle-sized congregation has its unique challenges and difficulties, so it also has distinctive strengths and signature contributions. These vary from one parish to another, even though they share the same size category. Despite these local idiosyncrasies, there are some advantages and strengths that are common to most midsize churches. We will now consider characteristics of these churches that contribute to the achievement of the priorities that God has assigned to the church. Interestingly, these strengths derive from the dynamics that the midsize church possesses due to its distinctive place as positioned between small and large parishes. While midsize churches may not necessarily be able to enjoy the best of both worlds, they are able to benefit from some of the characteristics of both small and large churches.

PROMISING ADVANTAGES OVER SMALL CHURCHES

The old adage of *bigger is better* is not universally true, especially when applied to the sizes of churches. Nevertheless, there are some potential advantages that the midsize parish has over the small one. The medium-sized church can capitalize upon these advantages and thus positively impact its members and the broader community. The following areas identify opportunities for the midsize church to excel in its mission and ministry, especially compared to a small church.

More People Resources
The first positive promise that a medium-sized church possesses is a strong pool of talented people to mobilize for ministry and mission. By definition, this size church engages more people than the small congregation. Thus it has at its disposal more human resources. An increase in people resources usually makes it possible for the midsize church to meet its basic survival challenges and to stretch into innovative and impactful efforts. "More congregants do not guarantee higher quality of ministries," Herb Miller maintains. "Small churches can also provide high-quality ministries. But a larger pool of people typically (a) broadens the range of gifts and graces with which to accomplish ministries and (b) adds the 'bench strength' of more individuals with those gifts and graces."[1] Compared

---

1. Herb Miller, *Church Effectiveness Nuggets, Volume 28: Coaching Midsize Congregations toward Positive Change* (N.p.: Herb Miller, 2009), 13.

to the small church, the increased number of people provides increased breadth and depth of human resources.

An increased number of people generally equates with greater breadth in the range of abilities, skills, interests, and aptitudes. These are gifts that God has given to his people, both by virtue of their creation and by virtue of the bestowal of the Holy Spirit upon them, to be used for the building up of the church. Accordingly, there is a broader talent pool from which the ministry of the church can draw. The Apostle Paul celebrates the breadth of this manifold and multiform grace of God (Rom. 12:3–8; 1 Cor. 12:1–31), as does the Apostle Peter (1 Peter 4:10–11). They also exhort Christians to employ these gifts and to celebrate their diversity as they are employed interdependently for the benefit of all and the advancement of God's purposes.

The cultural personality of a small congregation will often narrowly reflect the actual personalities and interests of the few members who compose it. But in a midsize parish the signature ministries are expanded because of the greater multiplicity of causes that are dear to its members and because of the larger pool of gifts and abilities which they bring to those causes. When pastors and lay leaders are able to identify such a mother lode of talent, this opens the possibility to *exploit* its riches in the most sanctified sense of that verb. A key strategy here is to develop a systematic process for stewarding these human resources so they are used for the building up of the church and for missional service to the community.

Furthermore, an increased number of people generally equates with greater *depth* of available people resources for any given initiative, effort, or program of the church. Not only are there more participants in ministry, but there is the potential for increased competence of lay leaders and volunteers. A baseball team that has depth in its pitching roster will stand a better chance of making it to the post-season. A military force that has greater depth in its personnel is more likely to succeed in its mission. An orchestra with depth in the musicians who play the instruments—e.g., first, second, and third violin—will excel in the quality of its performance. Likewise is a congregation more likely to prevail in its God-given vocation if it is able to draw upon a multiplicity of individuals who contribute to the endeavor.

In the medium church it is important to formulate and execute an intentional process for managing this depth of talent and people resources. One of the major differences between shepherding a midsize church compared to a small church is that the former requires the pastor to employ more management skills. Ways to address this need will be covered in subsequent chapters.

Enhanced Capacity for Outreach to the Community

A second asset that the midsize church typically possesses is a multiplicity of ministry offerings. A middle-size congregation should be able to

→ based upon a smny pool of talented people

provide significantly more ministry programs than a small church. This results from the greater number of interests and needs that members have and from the panoply of gifts and abilities that those members are able to exercise in order to advance their causes. This is a plus! This holds great promise! An increased number of service and outreach programs, properly aligned, affords strength and effectiveness to a congregation's mission and ministry.

Later in this book an entire chapter will be devoted to the subject of congregational programming. However, a few observations will be made here. First, the midsize church has the advantage over a small church in that it possesses greater potential to develop programs that reach beyond the walls of the church. It is more readily able to focus on mission and outreach to those outside of the church membership as well as on the basic needs of existing members. Many small congregations have the resources and initiative only to respond to the needs of members and to address the institutional issues that maintain survival. Regrettably, this is sometimes true of midsize churches as well. However, it need not be, since these larger congregations have more resources to expand into outreach as well as to provide care and ministry to the flock.

A higher capacity to develop quality programs provides the opportunity to attract newcomers. Excellent music and stylistic variety in worship may effectively engage visitors. Specialized educational offerings are advertised to the broader community and invitations made to non-members to attend. The youth program, women's auxiliary, and men's club are developed to involve participants in community service. Support groups attract the bereaved, divorced, and addicted both through formal external media and informal word of mouth. Subgroups of the congregation form missional communities that focus their efforts on serving a specific need in the surrounding neighborhood or in a relational network.

The midsize parish is able to reach out beyond its membership to serve those beyond its premises. It is able to connect with its neighborhood and civil community through outreach programming more readily than a small church can. Cynthia Woolever and Deborah Bruce, researchers responsible for the Congregational Life Survey that involved over three hundred thousand worshipers in more than two thousand congregations in the United States, report these findings from their research: "Surprisingly, mid-size congregations on average have larger percentages of people participating in social service groups, voting, giving to charitable causes, and expressing values supportive of a strong community focus than small congregations. What makes mid-size congregations turn to face their communities and see them more clearly? Perhaps the size is just right for maximizing the balance between a large enough pool of volunteers to draw on and a small enough community to discourage 'free riders,' members who enjoy the benefits of the faith community with little or no investment."[2] Middle-size churches are right sized for doing outreach into their neighborhoods and communities. In this regard their potential is very positive. *has been a request!*

Enhanced Capacity for the Nurture of Members

The medium-size parish will give attention not only to mission beyond its walls but also to the pastoral care and spiritual support of its own members. The multiplication of programs can facilitate this end. This size of church typically is able to offer a diverse educational program for all ages and for most stages in life. It is usually able to provide specialized ministry programming for children, youth, families, women, and the elderly. Sometimes it is able to expand to provide programs for young adults and men, as well as support groups for special needs such as those who are divorced, grieving, or recovering from addictions.

The midsize congregation frequently provides a higher level of quality in the presentation of its worship services than a small church. The musical offerings in worship involve more than one instrument and are delivered by musicians with some competence. Not infrequently there are multiple worship service times, with differing styles of worship in each service. The increased complexity of worship and musical programming requires more people resources, but it also provides increased opportunity for participation of lay volunteers who are gifted in music, the arts, and hospitality.

One area of particular strength for the midsize church is its ability to address the needs of families with children and youth. The findings of the Congregational Life Survey affirm this opportunity:

> Worshipers in small congregations are least satisfied with the programs for children and youth. They are least likely to list children's ministry as one of the three most valued aspects of their congregation. A smaller percentage of their children also attend the congregation. Mid-size congregations (with 100 to 350 in worship) score highest on two of the three factors—retention of youth and valuing the congregation's ministry for children. On the third factor—satisfaction with the congregation's programs for children and youth—large and mid-size congregations both exceed the scores of small congregations. Larger congregations, and particularly mid-size congregations, evidence greater strength in their ability to nurture and care for the future generation of worshipers.[3]

Because of the capacity of most midsize churches to develop programs that attend to the needs of members—adults, youth, and children—these congregations are able to retain members and serve them effectively.

2. Cynthia Woolever and Deborah Bruce, *Beyond the Ordinary: Ten Strengths of U.S. Congregations* (Louisville: Westminster John Knox Press, 2004), 69.
3. Ibid., 59.

In his pioneering work on the differentiation of churches according to size, Arlin Routhage identified the midsize church as the *program church*. Not only is the offering of a multiplicity of programs a distinctive characteristic of this size of church, it is a potential strength (if the programs are strategically aligned and competently executed), holding great promise for the flourishing of the parish.

Better Delivery of Care

Related to the increase of people resources is the possibility to provide more and better spiritual, emotional, and creaturely care to members of that community. This is the third potential advantage of a midsize parish. It is commonly assumed that the larger a church becomes the more impersonal is its cultural personality, and so the less effective is the network of personal care within the congregation. But that need not be the case. Indeed, there is great potential for more specialized and expanded pastoral care in the medium church.

In the family size church (15 to 50 worshippers) the members of this ecclesial family ordinarily will look after each other and deliver pastoral care to those who need it in an intuitive manner. The part-time clergy who leads this family flock also will be able to attend to those needs as they arise.

In the pastoral size church (50 to 150 worshippers) the burden of responsibility for delivering pastoral care rests solidly on the clergy leader, with congregational members assisting as they see the need. The pastor is able to manage the demands that result from the personal and spiritual needs of the flock.

However, in the medium-sized parish this becomes more challenging. Only in exceptional cases is the clergy leader able to attend to all the pastoral care needs of the members. But this does not mean that the midsize church cannot sufficiently provide pastoral care. Indeed, with thoughtful coordination of members' gifts and abilities, the church with 150 to 400 worshippers can excel in care ministry.

Because of the increase in human resources that a midsize church possesses compared to a small church, it has great potential to offer excellent personal care and to deliver it effectively. This size congregation typically will develop varied and multiple programs for addressing the needs expressed by members of the congregation as well as by the broader community. Usually this pastoral care becomes more specialized, providing support groups for various conditions such as those recently widowed or those suffering from addictions. These are agencies for the delivery of pastoral care that the small church usually is not capable of providing.

But also the more routine needs for pastoral care, such as visitation of hospitalized and homebound members, can be addressed quite effectively by staff and members of the midsize parish. The pastor of this size congregation should still be able to make such visits, although not as frequently as the pastor of a small church. But the pastor's visitation can be supplemented with that of lay members who have been equipped to provide empathic, meaningful care. A well-trained group of elders or deacons provides a significant pool for such supplemental service. Lay visitors and care-givers can be formed for this kind of service and given ongoing oversight and support.

Furthermore, middle-sized congregations typically recruit additional staff (paid and unpaid) beyond the pastor, whether full-time or part-time. These staff members will lead and direct program areas such as youth, music, and education. As leaders, they also can be equipped to provide spiritual care to people who participate in their areas of oversight and to be aware of and respond to these folks' needs of body and soul. This should include the willingness to listen to the burdens and hurts of people during the regular activities of their respective program areas. But it also involves proactive visitation of those who have critical needs, including hospitalization and confinement to home.

These care ministers—staff and lay—provide added value to the ministry of visitation and pastoral care of the ordained pastor. Frequently they will not only supplement the pastor's efforts but enhance care to those who are visited. The result is that the increased pool of human resources of the midsize church as compared to the small church is a real asset and advantage. Rather than being diminished, the potential for expanded availability and quality of pastoral care is increased.

Increased Diversity and Attraction
A fourth advantage of the middle-sized congregation over a small church is the potential for diversity to flourish. This is attractive to many in today's society. The potential for the midsize church to provide multiple program offerings and to deliver pastoral care in a breadth of venues increases its potential to attract outsiders and visitors as well as to expand the diversity of its membership.

The fact that the middle-size church has the capacity to serve a broader range of needs means that it is more likely to attract a greater diversity of people who seek to have those needs met. As such, it can appeal to different demographic groupings. Small congregations typically are very homogeneous, since their inclusiveness (feeling like family) often has the consequence of communicating to visitors that they are outsiders. It is more likely in a midsize church that people with diverse backgrounds will be able to find a place of inclusion in the multiplicity of program areas and ministry emphases. These areas and emphases become the initial context in which the new person identifies with the group, but eventually this identification extends to include the larger congregation.

There is still homogeneity in the midsize church, but it is located primarily in the various sub-groupings, programs, and mini-communities that constitute the congregation. These small homogeneous groups provide the context for individuals to find belonging and identity with like kind. But the fact that the groups are sponsored by and connected to the larger congregation provides opportunity for greater demographic diversity in the whole. This is healthy both spiritually and socially as it enables Christians to be stretched in their engagement with people who are different from them.

Typically the midsize church has more capacity than the small church to reach outward. The Barna Research Group claims that demographic and cultural forces are at work to keep small churches from growing, but this is not the case with medium-sized parishes. Indeed, Barna reports, midsize congregations have great potential to attract the demographic of upscale adults who bring more financial resources and a higher educational capacity to bear. This enables them to take more risks in marketing and outreach.[4] This is not to deny that midsize churches have other demographic constituents as well, including lower class members. But it does mean that frequently small churches lack members who are highly educated, highly paid, and entrepreneurial. Midsize churches are likely to be more diverse in the levels of education, income, and innovation than are small churches. This increased diversity gives medium churches an edge when it comes to creativity and imagination.

PROMISING ADVANTAGES OVER LARGE CHURCHES

In addition to having several advantages over the small congregation, the midsize church possesses some possible advantages over the large one. Although there are many characteristics of the midsize parish that distinguish it from the small church, there are also some areas of commonality. Accordingly, the medium church can capitalize on some of the advantages that are the result of being smaller than the large congregation. In the following areas the old adage of *less is more* applies, as the midsize church holds promise to achieve these values more than the large congregation.

Holistic Community
The first advantage to being smaller than the large church is that the midsize assembly is better able to cultivate an environment of warmth, friendliness, and care. In short, although the members of a medium church will identify with subgroups in which they experience belonging, fellowship, and intimacy, they also are able to have a sense of community with the entire congregation. Lyle Schaller characterized a medium congregation as follows: "There is a high degree of spontaneity behind the genuine caring for one another. Comparatively few members feel neglected or overlooked or ignored. It is small enough to offer the intimacy and

---

4. "Small Churches Struggle to Grow Because of the People They Attract," *Barna*, last modified September 2, 2003, https://www.barna.com/research/small-churches-struggle-to-grow-because-of-the-people-they-attract/.

friendliness that so many laypersons place at the top of their priority list in seeking a church home."[5] The midsize church holds great promise for fostering a spirit of holistic community among all members.

This environment is an intangible asset in an age in which many people, especially those of younger generations, are searching for authentic community. Despite the proliferation of opportunities for people to connect with one another through technology and online social networks, many remain lonely. American culture is highly individualistic, and this has taken its toll on people's sense of belonging and connection to community. Social scientists maintain that humans are predisposed genetically, physiologically, and psychologically to be attached to social communities. Christians understand that God created humans to be in community and has redeemed them to become part of the communion of saints.

Sociologist Robert Putnam demonstrated through research that during the final half of the twentieth century Americans became less socially connected.[6] This is manifested in the observation that their involvement in civic, religious, political, professional, and leisure organizations (such as bowling leagues) has declined precipitously. In the twenty-first century the proliferation of technological devices and electronic entertainment that demand an individual's attention—such as portable computers, internet access, streaming video, electronic games, smart phones, digital music players, etc.—has compounded this development. Many, especially of the Gen X and Millennial generations, have replaced face-to-face interactions with communication on the internet and via texting and social media.

Yet many people remain lonely. They are searching for trusting relationships and authentic community. Despite the opportunity to access others immediately and repeatedly through electronic communication, one dynamic is needed for the deepest form of authentic community— physical presence. This is the context in which relationships of intimacy, closeness, empathy, and depth can emerge and be nurtured. The biblical witness itself makes clear that God designed humans to be social beings who form genuine community in an environment of shared physical space, "We require people to interact with us (not our image), to call us to task, to encourage us, to uplift us, to share physical space with us. We need someone who can put his or her arm around us when we need comfort and who can extend a flesh-and-blood hand when we find ourselves alone. In short, we need someone to be Christ to us now."[7]

The midsize church provides a context for the cultivation of such intimacy and empathy. The Congregational Life Survey demonstrates that

---

5. Schaller, *The Middle Sized Church*, 103.

6. Robert Putnam, *Bowling Alone: The Collapse and Revival of American Community* (New York: Simon and Schuster, 2000).

7. Matthew Kobs, "Technology and Community," in *Inviting Community*, ed. Robert Kolb and Theodore Hopkins (St. Louis: Concordia Seminary Press, 2013), 191.

worshipers in medium-sized parishes have a greater sense of belonging in their churches than those who are members of large congregations. The researchers report that the overall score on the *Sense of Belonging Index* is higher in midsize churches (thirty-six percent) compared to large churches (thirty-two percent), and is almost the same as that in small parishes (thirty-seven percent).[8]

Although the cultivation of an ethos of intimacy and belonging may not happen as spontaneously and organically as in a small church, it can be promoted by proactive efforts on the part of the pastor and other congregational leaders. The pastor will regularly and repeatedly make public statements that encourage the members to share hospitality with and express concern for others (both members and visitors). Leaders—both clergy and lay—will model this warmth, approachability, friendliness, and caring approach, setting the tone for the social atmosphere of the congregation. A purposeful integration of new members will greatly promote this endeavor. Intentional efforts to connect people to belonging groups, support agencies, and service efforts in the congregation will go far in advancing an ethos of inclusion into the community life of the church.

The midsize church has great potential to offer an answer to the search for community among many people, especially those who are of the younger generations. Its many program offerings provide meaningful groups into which people can be integrated and within which they find a place of belonging. In this way it is like the large church. But it is unlike the large congregation in that members can still readily identify with the entire congregational community. This is a distinctive quality of the middle church that holds promise for the future. The Barna Research Group maintains that the medium congregation can attract younger generations (Busters and Mosaics) whose values and priorities align more with its size culture.[9] An emerging value among young Christians in America is the community dynamic that is characteristic of middle-sized parishes. These churches should capitalize on this opportunity by nurturing this strength.

Spiritual Formation and Ministry Involvement

Another asset of the midsize church which has potential to exceed the large parish is its capacity to cultivate spiritual formation and ministry involvement among its members and affiliated non-members. The Congregational Life Survey identified several characteristics of worshippers who are growing spiritually: their spiritual needs are being met in their congregation, they spend time in private devotional activities, they are growing in their faith through participation in activities of their church, and they value involvement in Bible study, prayer groups, and prayer ministry.

---

8.   Woolever and Bruce, *Beyond the Ordinary*, 49–50.
9.   "Small Churches Struggle to Grow," *Barna*.

This research demonstrated that midsize congregations score significantly higher on the *Growing Spiritually Index*—an overall score of forty-six percent—than large congregations (which had an overall score of forty-two percent).[10]

The midsize church generally is oriented toward programmatic development. This is why it is classically categorized as the *program* church. Members identify with and find a place of belonging in a specific program or affinity gathering. This could be a Bible study, parenting class, prayer group, couples' club, women's auxiliary, choir, praise band, missional community, or service organization. These affinity groups are contexts that have great potential to form faith and discipleship. The challenge, however, is to develop the content and quality of these programs, groups, classes, and ministries in a manner that is intentional and proactive. More will be said about this in the chapter on programming, but suffice it to say that this is an area for significant impact in the spiritual lives of believers, one that holds strong potential for the medium church.

An implication of a strong spiritual life is an increased willingness to participate in activities of the congregation that both nurture faith, such as parish education classes, and that enable members to respond in service and stewardship. Once again, research indicates that midsize parishes are more apt to promote this involvement of members than large churches.

The Congregational Life Survey indicates that middle-sized congregations have a larger *proportion* of members who participate in activities such as Sunday school, Bible study, or prayer teams than large churches. They also surpass large congregations in equipping members to practice financial stewardship. Furthermore, members are more likely to assume leadership roles in the congregation and to participate in its decision-making processes. The Congregational Life Survey indicates that midsize churches exceed large churches by over ten percentage points in the overall score of the *Participating in the Congregation Index* (fifty-nine percent to forty-eight percent).[11] The researchers report that, compared to large churches, the typical medium congregation has a higher proportion of members involved in small groups, decision making, leadership positions, and financial support.[12]

Therefore in the areas of ministry involvement and discipleship formation, medium-sized parishes in general have an edge over large congregations. This is a strength that should be maximized by such congregations! The promise is great for a midsize church to accomplish its God-given purpose to cultivate the spiritual lives of its members and to equip them to be faithful stewards and servants of the Lord in the world.

---

10. Woolever and Bruce, *Beyond the Ordinary*, 16–20.
11. Ibid., 40–41.
12. Ibid., 41.

SUMMARY

The middle-sized church is filled with promise. It has great potential to prevail in its mission. Leaders of this size parish will recognize the distinctive opportunities that the context affords, so that they may optimize the potential for fruitful ministry. Medium churches typically are presented with many distinctive opportunities to engage in fruitful mission and to provide meaningful ministry.

Compared to the small church, the typical midsize parish possesses several advantages. It has greater human resources that bring an expanded breadth of giftedness and an increased depth of participation. The program-size church typically has a multiplicity of quality ministry offerings that afford greater potential for outreach to the community as well as spiritual nurture for members. There exists the opportunity to provide more specialized and expanded pastoral care. Finally, the increased diversity that is typical of this size offers a much higher degree of heterogeneous engagement among members, while also making available contexts for homogeneous belonging.

Research such as that conducted by the Congregational Life Survey also indicates that the medium church demonstrates some advantages over the large parish. It typically provides a warmer and more caring corporate environment that is conducive to holistic community. It has a high capacity to cultivate spiritual formation and involvement in ministry among its members.

These distinctive qualities are typical of the middle-size church. This means that it has potential to carry out effectively the calling that God has placed upon it, especially if its disadvantages are minimized and its advantages are maximized. But what is that calling that God has for his church? How does a midsize congregation carry out this vocation faithfully and effectively? The answers to these questions, addressed in the next chapter, will give direction to the mission and ministry of the medium-sized church.

CHAPTER 5

PRIORITIES

Michelle Sanchez found great fulfillment in serving as a congregational officer of Faith Church. But sometimes she also experienced frustration in this role. One of those occasions followed a church council meeting. The previous evening she had participated in the gathering of chairpersons of the congregation's seven boards. The monthly meetings were meant to facilitate the coordination of activities within the congregation. But last night's meeting convinced Michelle that each board was mostly doing its own thing with little regard for the larger cause or purpose of the church. The image of a herd of cats seemed apropos—each cat was moving in its own direction. There appeared to be very little sense of movement together toward a common goal.

Over coffee later that day Michelle confided with her friend Sally the frustration she had with her task as a leader in Faith Church. "When I read in the Bible how it was said of the Israelites that 'everyone did what was right in their own eyes,' all I can envision is our own council members," she lamented. "It seems that each leader has his or her distinct agenda. Each board pursues its own direction without much regard for a unified movement." As a result, Michelle concluded, there was a lot of activity going on at the church without a commensurate impact for the larger kingdom of God.

Moreover, the boards and committees appeared merely to repeat past efforts without much reflection or assessment of effectiveness. They conducted these activities out of habit rather than for the sake of the church's purpose. "We do things simply because it's what we've done in the past. And we do it the same way since we've done it that way before. But no one really knows *why* we are doing it. We are lacking a unifying purpose to move toward."

Sally responded with a nod. Then she commented, "It sounds to me like your church is suffering from mission drift."

"Mission drift?" Responded Michelle, "What's that?"

"It is when an organization that once knew why it existed gradually over time loses that sense of purpose and focus," Sally explained. "It's like a ship that imperceptibly drifts off course. The organization slowly drifts away from its original purpose, from what it was meant to be and to do. It's not uncommon for an institution—even a church—to experience mission drift."

"That sounds like us!" Michelle replied. "So tell me more."

Sally sipped her coffee and continued. "The symptoms of mission drift are many. But usually it looks like this. There is a lack of clarity about why the organization exists. People are confused or apathetic about what they are supposed to be doing. As a result, resources are wasted—time, effort, and money. Furthermore, members of the organization develop their own ideas about what the group should be about, which leads to the formation of factions that move in different directions. Sometimes this misalignment of effort simply leads to indifference about what the other groups are doing. But oftentimes the factions find themselves at odds with one another, and conflict arises. In either case, over time the organization loses energy and forward momentum. There may be lots of meetings and activity going on, but this mostly serves to perpetuate the institution for its own sake rather than to advance the cause for which it was initially created."

"Doctor, you have diagnosed the condition we have at Faith Church!" Michelle exclaimed. "Mission drift—that's what is ailing us! But now tell me how it can be remedied!"

Sally looked intently at her friend. "Just as you didn't get to where you are overnight," she asserted, "you are not going to get back to where you should be overnight. It will take time. Remember the image I used earlier of a ship that has gotten off course. Well, you cannot turn an ocean liner on a dime! It takes effort at maneuvering to get back on track in the direction you should go. But although it may take significant effort, the solution really is simple. This is done by bringing your organization—in this case Faith Church— back to its priorities. First of all identify the few essential reasons for the church's existence. Then make these to be the church's priorities. They must be articulated in a clear and compelling manner as the most important endeavors of the church. Once clarity on these is achieved, commitment to them must be won. Lastly, in order to see that there is execution of the priorities, you must develop a comprehensive strategy that puts those priorities into practice in the efforts of your members."

"I can see why it is easier just to let the ship drift," Michelle sighed. "But that's not what we have been elected to do as a leaders of this congregation. And that's not what God would want us to do. So tell me, Sally, how *do* we identify what our priorities should be?"

Sally leaned back. "I'll tell you what you *don't* do to identify the priorities of your church, at least not initially. You *don't* simply ask people to give their opinions about what the church should be doing. Then you'll have the same situation as what you're experiencing now. Instead, you lead the people to examine what *God* says is the purpose of his church! Look at what God's word says the church is and what it should be focusing upon. Once that is established, you will be able to take the next step in discussing and agreeing on *how* to put the priorities into practice at Faith Church. That will move your church from mission *drift* to mission *shift*. But it all begins with the priorities God has for his church!"

GOD'S PURPOSES

Sally provided wise guidance to Michelle by encouraging her church to examine what God's purposes are. However, oftentimes when we hear about God's purposes, we immediately think of what God deems important *for us to do*. This matter will concern us in due time, but not immediately. The reason is because God's purposes begin not with what *we do*, but with what *he does*. God's purposes are seen supremely in what he has invested himself into.

Look at your own life. Your purposes and priorities are evident primarily in your own behavior. If work in your profession dominates your waking hours, then the advancement of your career is your *raison d'etre*. If you spend significant time while at home serving, supporting, and interacting with your spouse and children, then having strong relationships with family members is a priority. Should your life be dominated by a certain activity, this reflects what you perceive your purpose is. It can be as different as rigorous exercise is from watching television, as contrasted as praying is from partying.

So also, to discover God's purposes we must examine his behavior. What is it that he has devoted himself to? What has he invested his efforts into? By discovering God's activity we will better grasp what his purposes are for us!

This is where the ecumenical Christian creeds inform us. For centuries the Christian church has used these confessional statements as summary articulations of who God is and what he has done and continues to do "for us and for our salvation." The Apostles' and Nicene creeds do not speak about what we do, other than the prefatory statement of "I believe." The content of the creeds is thoroughly descriptive of what God does. The first article of the creed affirms God's creative effort as "maker of heaven and earth." The second article describes the saving activity of God the Son. The third article depicts the sanctifying work of God the Holy Spirit. Moreover, the primary movement of God the Son in the second article and God the Holy Spirit in the third article may be summarized with the word *down*. God's action in both cases is a downward mobility! He *comes down* in order to accomplish his divine will and purpose for human beings.

First of all, the mission and ministry of the midsize church is *God's*—he is carrying out his purposes and priorities! He has done so in the sending of his Son, Jesus. He continues to do so in the sending of his Spirit. And he does so now through the Spirit-indwelled body of Christ on earth called the church. He does so through us!

THE CHURCH'S PRIORITIES: GOD'S PRESENCE, POWER, AND PLAN IN THE WORLD

The second and third articles of the creeds depict God's activity as a downward mobility in order to bring God's presence, power, and plan into the world. In the second article, God the Son descends into human flesh in the person of Jesus of Nazareth and makes his *presence* among sinful human beings. He does this, as the Nicene Creed states, "for our salvation," since God's *plan* is to reconcile sinful people to himself and to restore fallen creation. Such reconciliation and restoration is beyond the strength of sinful humans, so the sinless God-man Jesus Christ accomplishes God's mission through the *power* of his atoning sacrifice on the cross and victorious resurrection from the dead. The second article is about God's presence, plan, and power to redeem us.

In the third article of the creed, God the Holy Spirit descends into human hearts and fills them with his sanctifying *presence*; Christians individually and corporately become the temple of the Holy Spirit. He does this to bring the *power* of Christ's atonement and resurrection to them, the gospel, which is the "power of God unto salvation" (Rom. 1:16). This empowers them through the forgiveness of sins to live sanctified lives of faith, faithfulness, and fruitfulness. The Spirit's *plan* is to form agents of God's saving and sanctifying work, bringing the life-giving word of God to others in the world. The third article is about God's presence, plan, and power to restore us.

These priorities of God which are evident in his downward activity now become the priorities of his church, the body of Christ in the world. These are the priorities of the church universal and of individual congregations. They should be the priorities of all churches, no matter what size. Although this book focuses on the mission and ministry of the midsize church, these priorities are shared with small congregations and large ones. They are universal priorities for the people of God in all churches. In subsequent chapters we shall see how the midsize church distinctively attends to these priorities. But it is essential to understand from the beginning what those priorities are.

PRIORITY ONE: BEARING GOD'S PRESENCE

Contemporary society places a high value on connectedness and community. People seek to be connected through personal relationships and social networks. This connectivity may be face-to-face or online with family and friends. At a deeper level, people seek to join communities in which they can know others and be known by others and experience belonging, closeness, and even intimacy. But in order for connectedness and community to happen, there first of all must be presence. Presence affords the opportunity for communion, and communion opens the possibility for community.

The Christian church offers community that is deeper than anything that secular society might provide. It offers union with God and participation in, as the Apostles Creed puts it, "the communion of saints." Contemporary notions of fellowship and harmony—of shared practices, language, and values—certainly are part of Christian community. But the community that is the church is more than that. It is a theological reality. It is the family of the Father. It is the body of Christ. It is the temple of the Holy Spirit. In the church, as a theological entity, the Triune God is present. Through the church, people are connected to God. They share communion with him and with others in his family. They are joined to a community that transcends racial, ethnic, national, and language demarcations. This is all because of the presence of God in their midst.

It is a priority of God to descend to be present among his people. The second and third articles of the creed shout this truth. This is God's mission, the reason the Father sent the Son into the world and the reason the Father and Son send the Spirit. It is to bring God's gracious presence to people, his visitation of reconciliation. But in order for the holy God to be present with his human creatures, that which hindered communion—the sinfulness of fallen people—needs to be removed. Accordingly, the Son took human flesh to bear sin and its curse as a substitute for sinful humanity. And the Spirit descends to bring the sin-cleansing merits of Christ into the lives of sinners today. God bestows the forgiveness of sins on those who acknowledge their need for such and trust their Savior. This restored presence of God brings reconciliation between the Creator and his human creatures. This is God's priority!

So what is the church's role in God's activity of reconciliation? The church—tangibly manifested in the lives of individual believers, gathered congregations, and trans-congregational associations—is God's agency to bring his gracious presence into the world. This vocation is clearly communicated by the Apostle Paul in his second letter to the Corinthians. He writes: "If anyone is in Christ, he is a new creation. The old has passed away; behold, the new has come." (2 Cor. 5:17). The idiom that Paul uses here, *in Christ*, is a favorite of his. It expresses in theological shorthand the concept of being united with Christ and his saving work—that is, to have the gracious presence of Christ and to receive his imputed righteousness. This presence is made possible by the downward mobility of God the Son and God the Holy Spirit depicted in the second and third articles of the creeds.

Paul proceeds to describe how the church participates in bringing the gracious presence of God into the fallen world so that those alienated from God by sin might be reconciled to him. "All this is from God," he writes, "who through Christ reconciled us to himself *and gave us the ministry of reconciliation*; that is, in Christ God was reconciling the world to himself, not counting their trespasses against them, *and entrusting to us the message of reconciliation*. Therefore, *we are ambassadors* for Christ, God making his appeal *through us*. We implore you on behalf of Christ, be reconciled to God" (2 Cor. 5:18–20, emphasis added).

In this passage the apostle interweaves what God has done in Christ and what he endeavors to do through those who are in Christ, the members of his church. God's priority in the sending of his Son to be present in this fallen world was to reconcile people to himself by the forgiveness of their sins. This was accomplished climactically and completely in the death and resurrection of Jesus. Yet this divine work of reconciliation has not been received by all; myriads continue to live in unbelief and in alienation from the Father. Thus to these God sends Christians to be his ambassadors of reconciliation and to deliver the message of reconciliation. "As the Father has sent me," Jesus spoke to his disciples, "even so I am sending you" (John 20:21).

Christians now join in the mission of God to bring the reconciling presence of God to others through the ministry and message of reconciliation in Christ. This is the gospel, of which we are ministers, messengers, and ambassadors. This is the priority of the church universal. This is the priority of churches—Christian congregations. So also this should be the priority of the midsize church—to bear God's *presence* for reconciliation.

PRIORITY TWO: DELIVERING GOD'S POWER

Power is defined as the ability to act or produce. There are many types of power in the universe today. We are familiar with mechanical and electric power in the physical realm. In the social sciences there are political, economic, and interpersonal powers. But when it comes to the "ability to act or produce," one power is preeminent—the power of the word of God. It is this power that brought all of creation into being, and thus is the source of all the created powers previously identified. In Genesis chapter one each repetition of the formula, "And God said…" is immediately followed by the effecting of what was spoken: light, firmament, seas, dry land, vegetation, heavenly bodies, sea-borne creatures, air-borne creatures, land animals, human beings. Of all the advances in science accomplished by humans, one remains elusive and beyond our power—the ability to create life from that which is lifeless. This creative power human creatures are unable to effect, for it remains the prerogative of God.

In terms of the second and third articles of the creed, God's word continues to demonstrate creative potency. This is especially evident in its power to bring life from death. Jesus Christ is God's Word incarnate—"In the beginning was the Word, and the Word was with God, and the Word was God…In him was life, and the life was the light of men" (John 1:1, 4). By his word, Jesus of Nazareth healed the sick, calmed the sea, and raised the dead. The Word made flesh—now risen from the dead—effects a new creation, so that "if anyone is in Christ, he is a new creation" (1 Cor. 5:17). Paul declares that "through the appearing of our Savior Jesus Christ," God has "abolished death and brought life and immortality to light through the gospel" (2 Tim. 1:10). The appearing of the God-man Jesus Christ brings life out of all kinds of death—physical, spiritual, and eternal.

The Holy Spirit, whom the Nicene Creed identifies as the "Lord and giver of life," continues to bring life from death through the word of God. First of all, the Spirit works regeneration through the word of the gospel. The Apostle Peter writes, "For you have been born again, not of perishable seed, but of imperishable, through the living and enduring word of God." (1 Peter 1:23). This word of God effects new life through various forms. In its oral form it is delivered through the proclamation of the message of the gospel, the story "that Christ died for our sins in accordance with the scriptures, that he was buried, that he was raised on the third day in accordance with the scriptures" (1 Cor. 15:3–4). In its written form the word of God continues to create and nurture life-giving faith as people read and study the scriptures (2 Tim. 3:15–17). In addition, the word of God is attached to simple water and to bread and wine, such word that pledges the new life of faith through baptism (John 3:5–7; Acts 2:38–39; Rom. 6:3–7; Col. 2:11–14; Titus 3:5; 1 Peter 3:21–22) and delivers nourishment for life through the Lord's Supper (Matt. 26:26–29; Mark 14:22–25; Luke 22:15–20; John 6:53–58; 1 Cor. 11:23–26). All of these are forms of the word of the gospel, which is "the power of God for salvation to everyone who believes" (Rom. 1:16). This is supreme power!

Christians have been entrusted with this power of God's word to bring life to a dying and decaying world. This powerful word in all of its forms is the means through which God's judgment of sin and vivifying grace is delivered to sinful humans. The word of God's holy law and righteous standards convicts sinners of their impotency to save themselves. The word of Christ's saving work then creates a reliance (that is, faith) in Jesus as their Savior from sin and its bondage. Moreover, it delivers power to those saved by grace so that they can lead lives that align with God's will expressed in his law.

Christians, and the churches that form and feed them, are thereby agents through which God the Holy Spirit effects his powerful life-giving work as they deliver God's powerful word. God's priority in this world is to create spiritual life in those who are dead in sin. His priority is to sustain and nurture that life by growth in faith. His priority is to deliver a life that is eternal—which even physical death cannot terminate—so that on the last day he will "transform our lowly body to be like his glorious body, by the power that enables him even to subdue all things to himself" (Phil. 3:21). These are the effects of the Lord's powerful word. These are his priorities.

As Christ's church and as servants of his word, we now join in this mission to deliver God's life-giving power "for the life of the world" (John

6:51). This is our priority. This is the priority of the midsize church—to deliver God's *power* for regeneration and life.

PRIORITY THREE: ACCOMPLISHING GOD'S PLAN

The sweeping narrative of Scripture depicts how the Creator has undertaken to restore his fallen creation. This divine activity of restoration is summarized in the second and third articles of the creed. Frequently Christians misunderstand God's purpose for humans as one of escapism—God delivers believers' souls from this corrupted world to a disembodied state in an ethereal heavenly destination. But the true end that God has for human creatures—indeed for all of creation—is not escape from this world but the restoration of the world. This is what the Bible refers to when it speaks of "the restoring of all things" (Acts 3:21; Matt. 19:28).

Just as the entire creation was cursed because of sin (Gen. 3:17–19), so also it will be restored to its original condition of blessed perfection through the work of Christ "that enables him to subject all things to himself" (Phil. 3:21). This is the Apostle Paul's emphasis: "For the creation waits with eager longing for the revealing of the sons of God. For the creation was subjected to futility, not willingly, but because of him who subjected it, in hope that the creation itself will be set free from its bondage to decay and obtain the freedom of the glory of the children of God" (Rom. 8:19–21). This is the ultimate hope of the Christian (Rom. 8:23–25). This is the end, or goal, for which we long—a restored "new heavens and new earth in which righteousness dwells" (2 Peter 3:13).

This *telos* of God's restorative activity, the new creation, is not only accomplished on the last day, although it will be ultimately and fully consummated at that time. It is being accomplished now through the work of the Spirit. By being united with Christ through faith, being "in Christ," a believer becomes a "new creation" (2 Cor. 5:17). This means not only that we are raised from spiritual death to life through God's act of regeneration by grace through faith (Rom. 8:11; Eph. 2:1–6; Col. 2:13), but we now also "walk in newness of life" (Rom. 6:4). This is what the Apostle Paul refers to as "to put on the new self, created after the likeness of God in true righteousness and holiness" (Eph. 4:24; Col. 3:10). This means that Christians embody the will of God and the gospel of Christ. By the power of the Holy Spirit, they live by faith and walk in the ways of the Lord. They follow the Lord as his disciples. And they seek to make disciples of others through the power of Christ's word (Matt. 28:18–20).

God's primeval plan for human beings, the crown of his creation, was that they represent him as his agents on earth to care for his creation (Gen. 1:26–31). This includes care for one another, as the term *helper* expresses (Gen. 2:18, 20). As sinners are made new by the work of the Spirit through the word of God, they are restored to this original purpose. Jesus Christ, the new Adam, entered human history "not to be served, but to serve," and he calls his followers to do likewise (Mark 10:42–45). Disciples of the Lord now live to serve others in the various vocational contexts to which God has assigned them—among family, friends, coworkers, neighbors, and fellow citizens. They especially are called to care for those who are in need (Matt. 25:31–47; Luke 10:25–37). Ultimately, they love their neighbors as themselves (Matt. 5:44; 22:37; John 13:34; Rom. 12:9; Col. 3:14; James 2:8; 1 John 4:7).

The needs of people to which the church attends are not only physical and material, although certainly they are that (see Acts 2:44–45; 4:32–37; 5:12–16; 6:1–6; 9:32–43; 1 Cor. 16:1–3; 2 Cor. 9:1–5; 1 Tim. 5:3–16; 6:17–19; Heb. 13:1–3; James 1:27; 2:14–17; 3 John 5–8). But the needs are especially spiritual—the need to be reconciled to the Creator (the priority of presence) and made alive in the Spirit (the priority of power). Accordingly, the primary purpose of the Christian church, and of its individual congregations and members, is to deliver the word of the gospel to others. This is the divine plan for us: to bring the word of God's redemption in Christ to those of all nations who do not yet know or believe it. This was the point of the proclamation of the word of God in varied tongues on the day of Pentecost (Acts 2:1–36). It also means that those who are regenerated by the Spirit continue to be formed in the faith and the truth of God's word through its various modes: proclamation, baptism, witness, apostolic teaching, the breaking of the bread (Acts 2:37–47). This wondrous vocation for extending God's redemptive care to the crown of his creation—human beings—is carried out by his agents who embody his mission. This is the purpose of the church, of congregations, of Christians. This is the priority that is advanced by leaders of the midsize church—to accomplish God's *plan* of restoration.

DOWN AND OUT

The work of God in this world is primarily downward. The Son of Man "descended from heaven…in order that the world might be saved through him" (John 3:13–17). The Holy Spirit "came from heaven" and brought the promised "power from on high" at Pentecost (Acts 2:2; Luke 24:49). We cannot ascend to God, so he has descended to us to bring his gracious presence and power and to work his gracious plan in our lives. These gifts of grace continue to be delivered to us through the word of the Lord in preaching, teaching, personal and group study of the scriptures, gospel witness, and the administration of baptism and the Lord's Supper.

The church is not only the recipient of these gifts. It is the agency for delivering the gifts throughout the world. Individual Christians are the agents of God's grace as they bear witness to the gospel, speak forth God's word, and serve the needs of others in the name of Christ. Christian congregations also become agencies through which God works reconciliation, regeneration, and restoration.

Accordingly, there is another direction at work in God's mission. It is an outward one. The church is commissioned to go into all the world and bring the word of the gospel to the nations (Matt. 28:16–20; Mark 16:15; Luke 24:45–49; Acts 1:7–8; 9:15; 26:15–18). As it has freely received, so now it freely gives (Matt. 10:8). The priorities of bearing God's presence, delivering God's power, and accomplishing God's plan are enacted in an outward motion. The work of God is done through two movements— down and out—as the church both receives his gifts of grace and service (descending from above) and then distributes these throughout the world (extending outward to others).

SUMMARY

The priorities of God are the priorities of his church—to bear God's gracious presence into the lives of people who had been alienated from him by sin (reconciliation), to deliver God's power to enliven those once dead in sin (regeneration), and to advance God's plan to care for the spiritual and physical wellbeing of his creation (restoration). These are the priorities of the whole church of all times and places. They are priorities to which Christians who assemble around God's word in local congregations of varying sizes attend. These are to be the priorities of the midsize church.

In subsequent chapters we shall see how the midsize church distinctively attends to these priorities in its programs, planning, and member participation. We will consider the application of these priorities to the efforts of the midsize congregation. The current chapter surveyed the priorities that God has entrusted to all churches of all sizes. Now we turn to focus again on the distinctive dynamics of the congregation characterized by 150 to 400 worshippers in order to understand its unique potential for carrying out God's priorities of reconciliation (bearing his presence), regeneration (delivering his power), and restoration (enacting his plan).

CHAPTER 6

PROGRAMS

Amy Washington invited her new neighbor, Sarah Anderson, to have coffee one Saturday morning. The Anderson family had recently moved into the neighborhood from another city and were settling into their new environs. Since they resided next door to each other, the Andersons and the Washingtons had become friends. In fact, Sarah often inquired of Amy about the community and neighborhood, asking questions such as, "What lawn care company do you recommend?" and "Where is the closest dry-cleaning shop?" Amy was happy to provide any advice that might help Sarah and her family adapt to their new environment.

Even more important was the relational connection and support that Sarah found in her new neighbor. Sarah valued the hospitality and friendship that Amy had extended to her as she made this geographic and relational transition. It was good simply to have someone in this new context of life whom she could consider as a friend.

As they conversed that morning, the topic turned to church involvement. Amy inquired, "Have you considered attending any church since you moved here?"

"Not really," Sarah replied. "In our previous location we belonged to a small church, but we haven't made finding a church a priority since we arrived here. There have been just too many other issues to deal with in getting settled. But we probably should start searching for a church. Tell me, Amy, where do you attend?"

"Our congregation is Faith Church on Maple Street," Amy answered. "Like your former congregation, it's not a very large church. But then I guess I wouldn't describe it as small either. It is kind of midway between large and small. We love it there. The pastor is very personable and his sermons are interesting and inspiring. There's a lot going on at the church."

"Really?" Sarah responded. "Tell me about it. What are some of the happenings at your church?"

Amy thought for a moment before speaking. "Well, for not being very large, our church has a lot of programs. Of course, there are the Sunday worship services—the early service is traditional in style and the late service is contemporary. The education hour between services includes graded Sunday school for the kids and a couple of Bible studies and topical studies for adults to choose from. That's just Sunday morning. But there are also activities going on during the week."

"My former church only had one worship service," Sarah commented. "We were too small to sustain a Sunday school. We had only one adult Bible study on Sunday morning, and another that was taught by the pastor during the week. Although our church was a close-knit group, there really wasn't much it could offer our children. So about all that we were involved in was the worship service once a week. What other programs does Faith Church offer?"

"Well, I'll describe what I am involved in, and then what my family members participate in. I love to sing, so I am a member of the adult choir. We sing about twice a month in the worship services, although our practice is weekly. Also I am involved in a women's group that meets over the lunch hour on Tuesdays. Right now we are studying the women in the Bible. I think it is important to serve the community, so I also volunteer about once a month in the church's mission mall, which is a room in the basement of our church that provides used clothing and household goods to needy folks in the community."

"That's great!" exclaimed Sarah. "You are really involved."

"Yes, I guess it is true. Plus there are the ways in which my family members are involved. Brad serves on the usher team on Sunday morning and attends a weekly men's Bible breakfast. One Saturday a month our church sponsors a servant event in the community that usually involves helping someone clean or repair their house or yard. Brad will participate in that on occasion, although not every time. Actually, that is where he is right now."

"What about your kids?" Sarah inquired. "How are they involved?"

"Well, they all attend Sunday school on Sunday morning. During the summer the younger two participate in vacation bible school. Jordan, our teenage son, attends youth group most weeks. He also plays on the church's basketball team that competes in a church league. Abigail, our middle-schooler, attends the weekly Confirmation instruction classes. And Derek, our little guy, participates in the Cub Scout troop that is sponsored by Faith

Church. He also loves to join his dad in helping at the servant events some Saturdays like today."

Sarah put down her coffee cup. "Those are a lot of activities that your family members participate in at your church!" she observed. "You are really involved! I am impressed with the number of programs and opportunities for involvement that your church offers. Our small church back home had nothing like that."

"You know, you're right," rejoined Amy. "There is a lot going on at Faith Church! I never really took much note of that. And I know that there are many other programs, classes, and events to which my family is not connected. I've never really counted all the ministry opportunities that our congregation offers, but it is significant! And you know, it all seems to just happen! But I bet that behind the scenes there is much effort to plan and coordinate all of those programs and activities. Sarah, you've helped me to come to a deeper appreciation of all that my church offers! It certainly does have many programs in which to get involved."

PROGRAMS! PROGRAMS! PROGRAMS!

Arlin Routhage was the first to assign the label of *program church* to the midsize congregation.[1] The title has stuck ever since. Indeed, this is part of its identity. The middle-sized parish is to a great degree defined by its programmatic orientation.

A congregation with an average worship attendance of less than 150 is able to be very relationally oriented. The family-sized church (15 to 50 average worshippers) operates as one large family, all of whose members know each other personally and engage with one another directly. The pastoral size church (50 to 150 worshippers) continues to be organically unified by the relationships that members have especially with the pastor. In both cases the dynamic orientation of the congregation is organized around these direct, face-to-face relationships. Most noteworthy is the unifying impact of such direct relationships. Either all the members know one another, or all the members are connected through their relationships with one person—the pastor, or both. As Alice Mann has observed, the family church may be group-centered and the pastoral church may be pastor-centered, but both of these churches are organically unified.[2]

Once a congregation passes into the transition zone of around 150 active worshippers, however, this orientation usually changes. The medium-sized parish becomes more like an organization than an organism. The increased number of people results in an increased complexity and variety

---

1. Routhage, *Sizing Up a Congregation for New Member Ministry*, 5, 23.
2. Mann, *Raising the Roof*, 13.

of relationships. The wholeness of the congregational system no longer is intuitively apprehended by its members. People's sense of belonging and identification with the congregation becomes directed toward subgroups in the congregation that in fact are programmatic entities.[3]

This is why in ordinary circumstances programs become integral to the church with more than 150 average worshippers. The variety and multiplicity of programs in the midsize church is a natural outgrowth of the need for people to connect with smaller communities and affinity groups. The sub-communities provide a sense of belonging and provide the context for relationship building. The programmatic efforts cultivate a sense of purpose as members participate in causes that are meaningful to them and to which they can contribute according to their giftedness. The resulting rich diversity of programs takes on an organizational culture that is different from the more homogeneous culture of the small church. A primary focus of the medium congregation is to organize its varied array of programs in order to engage a complex variety of people. The church's orientation must become more heterogeneous.

CONNECTION POINTS

The multiplication of programs in the medium congregation provides a multiplicity of identity groups to which members can connect. In other words, people's identification is not only with the congregation as a whole, although this is by no means lost. It is also with the various and specialized program groups that engage their interest. A member's sense of belonging is tied to a special program with which she finds an affinity as well as with the parish as a whole. Participants in the medium-sized church, both members and affiliated non-members, will identify with a small group, Bible study, Sunday school class, choir, youth group, service team, or missional community. They will find identity in the congregation primarily in roles or positions, such as that of a board member or usher, rather than in simply being a member of the whole.

This creates another point of distinction from the small church. Whereas the small pastoral-size church (less than 150 average worshippers) is *pastor-centered*, the midsize congregation is *group-centered*.[4] The congregation becomes oriented toward a plurality of groups, and these groups often are manifested as programs in the church. Gary McIntosh describes this orientation thus:

> The medium church actually functions as a collection of family groups—classes, circles, fellowships, clubs, or organizations—rather than an extended family group. In some cases the medium-sized church is simply an over-

---

3.   Ibid., 13.
4.   Ibid., 12, 14–15.

grown small church, but a true medium-sized church is a complex mixture
of numerous influential groups. The expansion of the medium church
into various groups is normally accompanied by corresponding programs
or ministries identified with these groups. The youth are tied to a youth
ministry, the women to a women's ministry, the young marrieds to a young
marrieds' Sunday school class, seniors to a seniors' program, and so forth.
The organizing principle is no longer one of relationships, as connected to
the extended family; rather, the organizing principle is the programmatic
orientation attached to the various groups.[5]

One programs to connect

One result of this programmatic orientation is that while members will
identify with special groups and programs in the church, and will generally
be able to have at least a casual acquaintance with each member of the group
and call each by name, they will not be able to know every person in the
entire congregation. They will be unable to address by name every one of
the other members of their parish. The reality is that for most members of a
medium church the primary mode of relating to the congregation is not to
the whole but to a part or parts (i.e., programs). This is a significant difference
from the relational network that one typically experiences in a small church.

In the conversation between the two neighbors depicted early in this
chapter, Sarah was impressed with the variety and number of programs
offered by Faith Church. She was struck by the intensity of activity that Amy
described. Upon further reflection, Amy was also impressed. She had not
taken note of this phenomenon in her church until now. Congregational
consultant Alice Mann draws a similar conclusion from her analysis of the
data from the National Congregations Study. In these findings "the impression of intense activity in the program church is verified. Most program-size
churches (about sixty percent) have at least ten ongoing classes for children
or adults; a similar proportion of program-size churches report at least four
other ongoing groups—besides committees and musical ensembles. About
seventy percent of program-size churches have at least two choirs or musical
groups."[6] Mann proceeds to note that the average midsize congregation
employs a similar number of functioning committees (i.e., from four to ten)
as the average large church does.[7]

All of this confirms the original appellation ascribed by Arlin
Routhage to the medium-sized congregation. It is a *program* church. Its
identity is distinctively tied to a programmatic orientation and organization. No wonder that as early as 1985 Lyle Schaller called the middle-
sized church "a congregation of groups, circles, choirs, organizations, and
cells."[8] As Herb Miller has observed, the priorities of the small church are

5.   McIntosh, *One Size Doesn't Fit All*, 29.
6.   Mann, *Raising the Roof*, 8.
7.   Ibid., 8–9.
8.   Schaller, *The Middle Sized Church*, 95.

with people, and those of the large church are with performance, but the focus of the midsize congregation is on programs.[9]

THE PERIL OF PROGRAMS

Before moving forward on this subject, one issue needs to be addressed from the start. The typical medium-size church is programmatically oriented. That is reality. But that can also be a problem. This orientation can be a dangerous pitfall in the church's God-given vocation of bringing God's gracious presence, his life-bestowing power, and his missional plan to people. The peril is that the programs become more important than God's presence, power, or plan, or than the people who are to receive these.

Reggie McNeal sounds this warning in his book, *Missional Renaissance*. His assessment is that many churches in North America have focused more on developing programs than on developing people.[10] McNeal's critique is that the programmatic orientation in congregations of all sizes has in fact diminished spiritual development and maturity in church members. This is because many churches focus on expanding programs simply to satisfy consumer appetites.

Another consequence of the programmatic emphasis, intended or not, is a mindset that discipleship is lived out exclusively in the context of church-sponsored programs. This disintegrates the spiritual experience of people so that they fail to see that following Christ is for all of life. This emphasis cultivates the false perception that Christian discipleship is limited to the times in which one participates in a church-sponsored program. In this vein a believer's functioning in the various arenas of the home, workplace, neighborhood, and community are excluded from the life of Christian vocation. "The program-driven church has created an artificial environment divorced from the rhythms and realities of normal life," McNeal opines. "Its claims that participation in its consuming activities will result in spiritual growth is [sic] preposterous."[11]

McNeal's critique may be justified. Oftentimes, programs in churches cater to people's self-serving needs as consumers rather than form them to be stewards of God's gifts, servants to others in need, and agents of the Lord for advancing his mission in the world. In addition, it is possible that church programs can become ends unto themselves. They become institutionalized to the point at which the primary purpose of the program is to perpetuate itself rather than to form the faith and to cultivate the fruitfulness of people. This is why some congregational programs are perceived to be cold, impersonal, and bureaucratic. Frequently the perception is not illusionary but real.

9.   Miller, *Navigating toward Maximum Effectiveness in Midsize Churches*, 11.
10. Reggie McNeal, *Missional Renaissance: Changing the Scorecard for the Church* (San Francisco: Jossey-Bass, 2009), 91.
11. Ibid., 93.

However, the problems identified here are not inherent to what it means to be a program. It is not inevitable that a church's programmatic orientation will lead to these errors. McNeal himself acknowledges that programs are not bad in and of themselves. He does not advocate the abandonment of programs. Instead, he proposes that congregations pay attention to the purpose and outcomes of the programs. "You don't have to abandon all your fine programs to pursue engagement with people's spiritual journeys," McNeal states. "You will likely even use available programs when creating a portfolio of activities designed to accomplish each pilgrim's quest. It's all a matter of beginning point and perspective. In the program-driven church, you begin with programs and look for people to make them happen. In a people development-driven culture, you begin with people and then use established programs or whatever else it takes to help them grow."[12]

The key to assessing the propriety and value of a church's program is not to determine whether it is self-perpetuating or sustainable or even successful in terms of numbers of participants. The key to assessment is whether it is accomplishing the priorities of the church described in the previous chapter. The questions to be asked and answered in this regard are these:

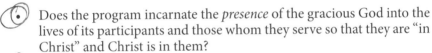

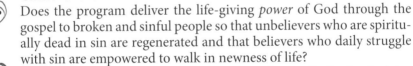

Does the program incarnate the *presence* of the gracious God into the lives of its participants and those whom they serve so that they are "in Christ" and Christ is in them?

Does the program deliver the life-giving *power* of God through the gospel to broken and sinful people so that unbelievers who are spiritually dead in sin are regenerated and that believers who daily struggle with sin are empowered to walk in newness of life?

Does the program equip its participants to advance God's *plan* by joining in his mission in this world so that creation is stewarded and human beings are restored to the wholeness that God intends for them?

Congregational leaders must continually ask such questions to assure that the programs are in alignment with the priorities that God has for his Church. A program is to be a means to an end, not the end itself. It should continually focus upon people and their spiritual development, faith formation, maturity as disciples, and vocational responsibilities in the world.

What are some principles for designing and developing a system of programs in a congregation that aligns with these priorities? What are some dynamics that accompany the programmatic orientation of the midsize church? It is important to identify these dynamics for the development of programs, which is ultimately for the development of people as they experience the presence, power, and plan of God in their lives.

---

12.   Ibid., 99.

WHAT'S THE NEED?

Visible mission

If a program exists for the sake of people (as it should), and not the other way around, then it must be concerned with what people need. Identifying and addressing people's needs has several implications.

First, the Bible tells us that the primary need that people have is to be restored into a right relationship with God (2 Cor. 5:17). They are to be reconciled to God through the atoning work of Jesus Christ and the justifying work of the Holy Spirit. This means that they have a need for righteousness *coram Deo*, before God. Thus the primary end of the programmatic efforts of a congregation is to deliver the word of the gospel to sinners so that they may believe that word and be right with their Creator, having peace with God (Rom. 5:1). This does not mean that every programmatic component of the parish will have this as its primary purpose. For example, some programs may focus primarily on serving the physical needs of people. But it does mean that cumulatively the priority of the programmatic effort is to deliver the righteousness of Christ to sinners through the message of the gospel.

Second, people need to be restored in their relationships with each other. There is much brokenness in the horizontal relationships of people because of sin and selfishness in their lives. Accordingly, the Christian congregation will develop programs that address these needs and channel the restorative power of God's love into broken relationships. This could be cultivated through cell groups, support groups, recovery initiatives, missional communities, and the like. It could be done through work-shops, courses, or retreats that help people live in *shalom* with each other in their marriages, families, friendships, workplaces, and other contexts of everyday living.

Third, people are physical creatures who have physical needs. Their bodies need to be fed, clothed, housed, and healed. Orthodox Christianity does not eschew the value of the physical body in favor of some disembodied spirit, as Gnosticism does. Christians care for the bodily needs of their neighbors both within and outside of the church. This is part of the horizontal righteousness that God calls his people actively to demonstrate to others. Martin Luther famously quipped that God does not need our good works, but our neighbor does.[13] Accordingly, the church organizes itself to provide for these creaturely needs of others. Oftentimes it does so through programs.

Lastly, people need to exercise the gifts they have received by giving to others. Jesus himself is quoted as saying, "It is more blessed to give than to receive" (Acts 20:35). We are created not only to receive from God and others, but to give to them. God has designed each person differently in their capacity to give. In fact, the Bible says that we give as a response to

---

13.   Gustav Wingren, *Luther on Vocation*, trans. Carl C. Rasmussen (Evansville, IN: Ballast, 1994), 10.

being given gifts—specifically the gifts of the Spirit that enable us to serve the common good and edify others (1 Cor. 12:1–31). This means that the church will organize its programmatic efforts in ways that maximize the giftedness of members. It will afford them with opportunities to exercise their gifts and talents and so fulfill the call to contribute of their own lives.

This dynamic of addressing people's needs takes discernment, however. In the first place, we must heed the caution articulated by Reggie McNeal and others and be careful not to capitulate to the ethos of consumerism in our culture. This is a pitfall that occurs when a congregation attempts to meet people's felt needs primarily for the purpose of attracting them in order to achieve the standards of success in this world—more customers, more dollars, more glory. Churches also should avoid simply catering to people's selfishness. Furthermore, just because there are needs existing in the congregation and community does not mean your specific parish is required to address each one. Just as human creatures are finite, so also congregations made up of humans are limited in resources and time. The congregation will have to prioritize which needs to attend to.

In its task of choosing which needs are addressed and which are not, one advantage that the middle-sized church has over the small church is a greater abundance of resources. This is especially true regarding human resources, as was demonstrated in the chapter on *promise*. Small churches are able to offer only a few programmatic efforts and a very limited selection of opportunities for involvement. But since the mid-size church is larger, it is able to accommodate a more diverse and multiplied array of opportunities in which members may be involved.

Furthermore, these programs can become more specialized. Typically the small church will have only a few standing boards, such as the elders, deacons, and trustees. But the middle-size church will in its ongoing structure perpetuate multiple program committees, including standing boards (for education, youth, outreach, worship, etc.) and task forces. In addition, this size of congregation is able to develop and sustain special initiatives such as support groups, recovery programs, mission teams, and small group fellowships. The parish possesses a sufficient critical mass to implement these. Gary McIntosh provides the following illustration of this principle: "A smaller church may have only one or two families dealing with alcoholism. While the church leaders are no doubt concerned for the special needs of the two families, there is not sufficient critical mass to offer a small support group or specialized class for them. As a church grows larger, however, it will soon have a number of families dealing with alcoholism. With the increased critical mass, the church will be able to offer a support group and/or special needs class aimed directly at this particular concern."[14]

---

14.   McIntosh, *Taking Your Church to the Next Level*, 185–86.

As was said earlier, the midsize parish cannot accommodate all the wishes and perceived needs of its members or community. It cannot be all things to all people. But it is able to address a significant number of these and do so with effectiveness and quality due to the larger pool of human resources from which it can draw.

THE BYPRODUCT OF BELONGING

The congregation should undertake to develop programs in order to serve the needs of people. That is the first level of benefit resulting from the programs—people are served. But there is a second level. Those who participate in the congregation's programs will develop a sense of belonging to the group in which they are involved. As noted earlier, members in a midsize church typically identify as much, if not more, with the programs in which they participate than with the plenary congregation. Timothy Keller observes that "in the medium-sized church, the primary circle of belonging is usually a specific affinity class or program."[15]

The significance of this must be emphasized. People remain active in congregations when they sense that they belong and have a relational tie-in. This dynamic has variously been identified as *assimilation, incorporation*, or *acculturation*. Whatever the label, the impact is undeniable. It is a relational glue that adheres people to the church. Folks will remain engaged with others when they believe that they belong with them. They sense that they are a part of that group's *koinonia*. This sense of community occurs when they experience mutual trust, relational support, and emotional safety within the group. Thus the programs exist not only to advance a cause or to address a need. They exist as contexts in which relationships of mutual trust, support, and security are fostered. In other words, there is a relational dimension to the program as well as a task outcome, and frequently the former is more important than the latter.

In the medium-sized parish the primary seedbed for this sense of belonging is in the various programs that are offered and available. Staff and lay leaders will be wise to give attention to this distinctive dynamic of the midsize church so as not to lose members through the back door but rather to cultivate their perception of the church as a place of belonging.

THE CHURCH OF PERPETUAL VITALITY

Not only do programs provide a kind of relational glue in the middle-size church, they also provide glue for the perpetuation of the congregation's ministry. The programs serve as a tangible framework for the continuation and stability of a congregation's mission, vision, and values. In general, this is more the case for the midsize parish than for small or large congregations.

---

15.   Keller, *Leadership and Church Size Dynamics*, 10.

In any healthy social organization the members must have a sense of stability. They seek to put their trust in that which is permanent, constant, and proven. This is why businesses with a proven track record succeed and why families with rich traditions flourish. In a church, people also seek constancy.

In the small congregation, a sense of constancy is maintained through the influence and leadership of a dominant family or families that hold an almost dynastic influence on the life of the church. Typically the tenure of a pastor in a small church is short, usually five years or less. The result is that the clergy office is viewed by the members as transient. Pastors come and go, as do their personal emphases and priorities. But the dominant extended family remains rooted permanently and so serves as the force for continuity in the congregation. For this reason usually the patriarch or matriarch of the key family in a small church will possess more power—either officially or unofficially—than the called pastor.

In the case of the large church the opposite is true. The senior pastor plays a critical role in the way in which members perceive the strength, vitality, and stability of the church. A large church requires effective executive leadership. The pastor's ability to cast a vision and align people to it is disproportionately more influential in a large church than in one that is of small or medium-size. This is why short pastoral tenures in large congregations are very destabilizing. Long tenures of the senior pastor (and to a lesser degree other professional staff workers) contribute significantly to the ongoing social stability of the large church.

But the midsize church is different. In this size of parish the programs provide much of the sense of permanence to members. This does not discount the important roles that the ordained clergy leader or other staff members play in reinforcing the sense of continuity in a congregation. But this is less true in the medium church than in a large church. The reason is because the programs of the midsize church serve not only as its organizing dynamic but also as a stabilizing force.

These programs can take the form of standing boards or committees in which leaders pass in and out of office, all the while its organizational structure remains. This dynamic may be evidenced in the ongoing ministries to children, youth, women, and men. For example, many midsize churches have women's missionary auxiliaries that have been in existence for half a century or longer. Programs that exert an extraordinary stabilizing influence include church-sponsored parochial elementary schools and to a lesser degree music ensembles and youth groups. Participants in these programmatic ministries are oftentimes highly invested in them. Although these folks may eventually end their participation, such as when the children graduate from the day school and their parents no longer attend school activities, the line of continuity continues in younger children who enter the school and their parents who become active as a result. These programs thereby perpetuate themselves and provide continuity and stability to the life and vitality of the midsize congregation.

POWER POINTS

James Davison Hunter, a prominent scholar of the relationship between social theory and religion, argues that power is inherent to any social group, including the church. "The church certainly is community, fellowship, and gathering," he contends, "but it is also an institution, and institutions, by their very nature, possess power and exercise power. . . . Thus, as long as the church is constituted by human beings and is a human institution, it will participate in the structures of power at work in the world and will exercise a power that is spiritually and ethically ambiguous at best."[16] This reality is not necessarily to be lamented. Davison takes issue with those who claim that exercising power is inherently evil and that powerlessness is somehow virtuous. In order for human beings to function in relationships with one another there must be the exercise of power.[17] The issue is not *whether* Christians and churches will exercise power, but *how* they do so.

For our present purposes we will take to heart Hunter's assertion *that* power is exercised in churches, and leave for another time *how* it is administered. The point to be emphasized here is that in the midsize parish the exercise of power is located primarily in its groups and programs and those who lead them. Herb Miller identifies the program leaders as the primary power brokers in the midsize church.[18] This contrasts with the small church in which the locus of power lies with the heads of the dominant families (patriarchs and matriarchs) and with the large church where the senior pastor and professional staff exert the power most effectively.

Power is vested with those who—officially or unofficially—exert influence and make decisions that impact the future of the organization. Thus those who make decisions exercise power in the church. In the midsize congregation, decisions are made more locally in program areas. In the small church decisions are made (or at least ratified) in the regular and relatively frequent plenary gatherings of the members. In this context the voice of the key families holds sway. In the large church decisions are made by those to whom decision-making has been delegated—the governing board and the professional staff (especially the senior pastor). In this context broad involvement of the congregation's members in the regular decision-making process is necessarily restricted. But in the medium church, the contexts in which decisions are made and thus power is practiced are in the programs and groups that are doing ministry.

---

16. James Davison Hunter, *To Change the World: The Irony, Tragedy, and Possibility of Christianity in the Late Modern World* (New York: Oxford University Press, 2010), 182.
17. Ibid., 177. Here Hunter coins the ascription to humanity as *homo potens*, "powerful man," to emphasize the inherent necessity of power to human social relationships.
18. Miller, *Navigating toward Maximum Effectiveness in Midsize Churches*, 16.

Officially in the middle-sized congregation, leadership power resides in standing boards and committees. This includes program boards such as those overseeing education, youth, worship, and outreach. In this case each board or committee is authorized to determine how its assigned areas of responsibility will be executed in the name of the congregation. Usually general goals or outcomes are provided to the boards that derive from the bylaws or the larger church council. These serve as a guide to the strategic direction that the body takes. But within these broad directives the group has significant latitude and freedom to make decisions on how it undertakes to achieve those goals. This is why decision-making is more localized in groups within the midsize church.

Typically the organizational structure of such a church will involve an overseeing entity such as a coordinating (administrative) council. This body is composed of representatives from each of the program boards of the congregation. For example, the elected directors of the education, youth, worship, and outreach boards will attend the meetings of the council. These leaders gather for important purposes, but oftentimes significant decision-making does not occur at this level. The reason is because the primary purpose of the gathering is to coordinate decisions that have already been made at the board or program level. Whether or not this is the best approach is debatable. But the reality is that it usually is the way things work in the medium church. What is important is to recognize that official decision-making is primarily located at the level of the various program boards and committees.

Of course, decisions are made in other groups as well. In the quarterly gathering of Sunday school teachers decisions are made about the format, curriculum, schedule, and approach for teaching the lessons. In the gathering of musicians for the praise band not infrequently the music leader seeks input from the other performers and decisions are made by consensus. Quite apart from the decisions of the Youth Board, the teenage members of the youth group collaborate to innovate activities and projects. And of course everyone knows what decisions of gravitas are determined in the parish kitchen while food is prepared and dishes are washed!

This system of decision-making that occurs in program groups poses a challenge to congregation-wide strategic alignment. The scheduling and coordination of activities that are promoted and carried out by the various groups oftentimes can be messy.

However, there is an upside to this more localized arrangement. Usually the members of these program groups are so close to the issues of need that decisions are owned by those who make them. Furthermore, the decision-making process is fairly nimble and reflexive. Participants in the programs as well as those who lead them recognize the need for change and redirection relatively quickly. Gary McIntosh affirms that not only are most decisions in the middle-sized church made by committees and program groups, but these entities are appropriately aware of the changing needs of the congregation and can adapt. He writes that "decisions about adding volunteers, hiring more staff, dealing with increased complexity, motivating stewardship, coordinating facility usage, or establishing policies are often *driven by changing needs*. Since the leadership power resides in boards and committees, this is where new ministry ideas originate, and the major decisions are hammered out and agreed on before they even go to the congregation for confirmation."[19] Thus there is ample opportunity for broad-based innovation and creativity among those who participate in the programs of the midsize congregation.

LEADING CHANGE

The corollary to this dynamic is that not only are programs the locus for decision making in the medium church, they are also the locus for change. McIntosh describes this as change occurring from the *middle out* through key committees. In the small church, McIntosh maintains, change is initiated and executed from the *bottom up* through influential members of the dominant families, such as the patriarchs and matriarchs. In the large church the catalyst for change is the staff team led by the senior pastor and the governing board. Thus change develops from the *top down* as it is conceived, launched, and executed by the professional staff in coordination with a few lay leaders. But the middle-sized church operates from the *middle out*.[20] The seedbed for change is in the boards, committees, and program groups that operate midway between the grass roots of lay members and the superstructure of the professional staff and the lay administrative council.

What this means is that ordained and lay leaders of midsize parishes who wish to promote change initiatives should give significant attention to relevant programs when facilitating the change process. One of the most widely accepted processes for leading change, as articulated by John Kotter, advocates that early in the process the leader must gather a guiding coalition to support and move forward the change.[21] In the medium church the best place to locate and recruit such supporters for the guiding coalition is in existing programs. This *middle out* approach effects beneficial change as program leaders, board chairpersons, and committee leaders take ownership of new initiatives.[22]

This dynamic has a flipside, though. Not only are programs the catalysts for change in the midsize church, but frequently the locus for *resistance* to change will be among those affiliated with a specific program in the church. If the members of these groups believe that the culture and

---

19.   McIntosh, *One Size Doesn't Fit All*, 75.
20.   Ibid., 99–101.
21.   John Kotter, *Leading Change* (Boston: Harvard Business School Press, 2012), 53–68.
22.   McIntosh, *One Size Doesn't Fit All*, 100.

values of their gathering is threatened by the initiative, they will respond by pushing back. Oftentimes pastors, staff, and lay leaders expect that in order to advance a proposal for change the promotional communication should be directed to the entire congregation. That is certainly necessary, but it is not enough. Directed conversations should be made with key participants in committees, teams, programmatic areas, and ministry groups (such as choirs or a women's auxiliary) who have a stake in the change. By convincing these key stakeholders of the value of the proposal, support will likely trickle down to the others in their constituent groups.

There is good news for leaders who wish to promote change in middle-sized congregations. Such churches typically are more accepting of and adept to change than small churches. "This does not mean that change is *easy* in midsize churches," Herb Miller notes. "However, change is easier to discuss because of more *group venues*, such as committee and Sunday school classes, in which such discussions can naturally occur."[23]

The old saw that the only change churches see is that in their offering baskets need not be the case. Middle-sized congregations are able to change, and to do so in a positive direction, if led effectively. Leaders of such parishes will be wise to capitalize on the distinctive dynamic of the midsize church— its programmatic components—to facilitate purposeful change.

SIZING UP PROGRAMS

One final comment must be said about the programmatic dynamic that characterizes the medium church. The fact is that program groups will differ from one another. Of course, the foci of the programs will vary. Some programs will focus on education, others on outreach, some on community service, still others on fellowship. Programs will also address varying constituents, including youth, young families, older adults, women, men, those with addictions, and so on. These are all significant, and somewhat obvious, distinctions between the groups.

But there is another especially important distinction that is frequently overlooked. That is the *size* of the programmatic groups. Even as size matters regarding entire congregations, so also size matters regarding the programs in those congregations. A taxonomy of constituent groups appropriate for the medium church is that developed by Theodore Johnson, who defines what he calls three basic building blocks of congregations.[24]

The smallest block is a small group of up to fifteen members. This is the context in which relationships of intimacy and care are best cultivated. Such small groups are composed of people who gather for study, prayer, encouragement, support, care, and service. These groups display

23. Herb Miller, *Coaching Midsize Congregations toward Positive Change*, 14.
24. Theodore Johnson, "Current Thinking on Size Transitions," in *Size Transitions in Congregations*, ed. Beth Ann Gaede (Herndon, VA: The Alban Institute, 2001), 17–24.

remarkable homogeneity as their members gather for shared concerns and needs (for example, a small group of young mothers who meet regularly to encourage and support one another in their common calling of raising small children).

The second building block that Johnson identifies is the family group, composed of fifteen to fifty participants. A characteristic of this group is that it is typically intergenerational and functions as an extended family or tribe. Leadership in a family group is more formalized than in a small group. Leaders are appointed or elected because they have proven themselves capable. Examples of family groups in midsize congregations are the choir, Sunday morning adult Bible class, the women's auxiliary organization, and a missional community. The family group is more heterogeneous than a small group, bringing together people of different generations, ages, gifts, backgrounds, and social standings. What unites them is a common interest or cause.

The third building block is the fellowship group, composed of 50 to 150 members but usually settling at about 100 participants. These groups gather almost exclusively for worship. Johnson observes that most midsize churches have less than 150 in attendance at each of their multiple worship services.[25] For example, the 8:00 A.M. traditional service serves as one fellowship group and the 10:30 A.M. contemporary service serves as another.

Johnson maintains that the family-sized church (10 to 50 worshippers) typically functions as a stand-alone family group and the pastoral size church (50 to 150 worshippers) functions as a stand-alone fellowship group. However, the midsize program church (150 to 400 worshippers) is composed of each differently sized category—small, family, fellowship. Johnson observes that typically a medium church will support ten to twenty small groups, ten or less groups in the family category, and two or three fellowship-size groups. Moreover, these varied sized groups are assembled variously in different congregations.[26] This explains why the midsize church is significantly more complex than the small church.

Staff and lay leaders of midsize parishes should recognize the dynamics regarding this diversity and complexity among the programs in the congregation. It is desirable for the church to cultivate these different types of groups in its programmatic design, for a midsize congregation composed of all three types of building blocks is a stronger church, sociologically speaking (and most likely spiritually as well). In fact, members who participate in all three levels of groups most likely will be soundly connected to the congregation.

A pastor should encourage members to be involved in at least two of these three types of groups. The shepherd should also give special attention to those members of the flock who are involved at only one level, for they are

---

25.   Ibid., 21.
26.   Ibid., 23–24.

at greatest risk of dropping out of participation in the life of the congregation. Parishioners who are involved in small groups will experience a high degree of intimacy and accountability with their comrades in the groups. Those participating in family groups will find themselves associated with a cause in which they can exercise their gifts and make a difference for Christ. And members who regularly gather to worship in one of the larger fellowship groups that are worship services will be nurtured with God's word and will form a greater vision of the larger community of the church.

SUMMARY

The midsize church is characterized as the program church. Its orientation is predominantly toward programs. There exist distinctive dynamics of the programmatic nature of the medium-size congregation. These dynamics have significant influence on how the programs of a congregation operate and function.

Ordained and lay leaders will recognize and engage with these dynamics in order to maximize the benefit of programs to people. As such, the programs are organized not for their own sake but for the sake of serving people. The programs become contexts for involvement and belonging of members and non-members, which in turn provide a kind of relational glue in the church.

The programmatic orientation of the midsize church offers a tangible framework for both stabilizing and perpetuating the congregation's mission and values. Because programs can serve as power centers, decision-making and leadership is exercised in them. Accordingly, programs are the primary locus for change (or resistance to it) in medium-sized parishes. And different sizes of programs themselves operate according to different dynamics. All of these are important factors in the operation of the typical midsize church. All of these are matters that leaders of medium churches do well to address.

The professional and lay leadership of the parish should be aware of these dynamics and engage them in ways that maximize their potential for good. But this implies that in fact the congregation has in place professional and lay leaders. The next several chapters will focus on the development of such leaders, whether they be staff or volunteer. No leader is more critical to the healthy functioning of the midsize church than the pastor. So it is to the pastor's role that we now give attention.

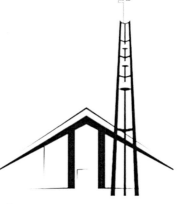

Congregational Round Table

This is our time together to dream and contemplate future needs at St. Paul. Here's some of the questions we want to think about:

1   It seems that the 8:15 a.m. Sunday start time has been a positive change due to the social time and educational hour between services. Do you have any comments regarding this?

2   In general terms, what would you like to see St. Paul undertake in the next 1, 5 and 10 years?

3   Do you feel that our current facility (worship, educational, community space) meets our needs? If you feel it does not, what specific changes, enhancements or expansion do you feel should be addressed?

4   Do you feel that alternative solutions should be investigated before facility changes are considered? Can you suggest ideas here such as additional service time offerings, additional staffing, or other thoughts?

5   Do you have other thoughts to share?

CHAPTER 7

PASTOR

Pastor Andrew Burke reflected upon the past four years in which he had shepherded the flock at Faith Church. The move from being the pastor of his previous parish, a small one, to this midsize congregation had been a challenging transition. It required him to make significant professional and personal adjustments.

As a seminary student Andrew had learned much about preaching, teaching, and providing pastoral care in ministry. This training served him well in the first two congregations he served. Both of these churches were small. In addition to his weekly responsibilities of leading worship and preaching, Andrew had regular opportunities to directly teach all the members of his flock. He catechized young members in the Confirmation course, and he instructed the occasional newcomer to the congregation in the Adult Information Class. He also taught the Sunday morning adult Bible study, a Tuesday morning Bible breakfast gathering of men, and a Thursday afternoon thematic study with a gathering of older women.

Pastoral care of the members was a priority for Pastor Burke in those early years. Whenever a member was hospitalized, Andrew visited them every day. The half-dozen homebound members received a visit from their shepherd every month. Pastor Burke committed to visit every household of the parish during the first year of his pastorate during those first two assignments to small churches. He attended almost all of the meetings of his congregation. Whenever the church held a special event, Andrew was there. Simply put, in his previous two congregations Pastor Burke was personally involved in the vast majority of their gatherings, events, and efforts. He enjoyed being in direct relationships with all of the members of these churches, and he loved interacting with them in all of their activities at the church.

But that changed when he took the reins at Faith Church, a parish significantly larger than his previous two congregations. Andrew quickly discovered that he was not able to have the kind of in-depth relationships with all of its members that he had enjoyed in the other churches he had served. He also was not able to involve himself personally in all of Faith congregation's activities. It was not that he didn't want to do this. He was simply not able to. He didn't have the time or capacity to do so. The opportunities for his direct involvement seemed infinite, but his energy was finite.

The many programs and activities at Faith Church demanded that Pastor Burke demonstrate skills different from those with which the seminary had invested him. They demanded a competency that was different from what he had demonstrated—with great success—in small churches. Although it was not technically a large congregation, Andrew discovered that Faith Church demonstrated a complexity that was disproportionately greater than that of the parishes he had served before. For one thing, the administrative responsibilities expanded exponentially. Furthermore, he was not able to attend all or even most of the meetings and events sponsored by the church.

This new normal for Pastor Burke gave him much stress and many feelings of inadequacy. He believed that he should know every member of his flock deeply, but even after a couple of years he had only a passing acquaintance with many of them. Certainly he was not able to make an annual visit to all of these people in their homes. Even the hospitalized members he visited every other day, not daily as was his practice in his previous contexts. The number of homebound members approached two dozen, and he found that making a personal visit to each of them once a month was a formidable challenge. In the other congregations where he had ministered Andrew felt he was on top of things. But during his first couple of years at Faith Church he was floundering. He lamented that he did not fulfill his vision of what a genuine caregiver of the flock should be.

The solution to this dilemma seemed to be to add staff to oversee some of the ministries of the church. Surely these coworkers would lighten Andrew's load by handling some of the programmatic functions! First a part time worker—a Service Gifts Coordinator—was contracted for fifteen hours a week to promote the active involvement of all members. Later other part-time positions were regularized, including a Director of Music Ministry and a Youth Director, each of whom were contracted for fifteen hours a week.

These additional staff positions led to the improvement of these ministries, but they failed to allow Pastor Burke to expand his one-on-one pastoral care functions. In fact, he now engaged more deeply in the managerial functions of overseeing the staff members. Time was spent in staff meetings and one-on-one sessions with each staff member. The administrative activities of delegating, supervising, and evaluating were added to his plate. Andrew assumed the role of head of staff at the church, and it seemed that this position's attendant administrative responsibilities were legion. His seminary education had not prepared him for this!

As a result of these developments, Pastor Burke experienced an identity crisis. "Who am I?" he pondered. "What am I supposed to be doing? What is my role as a pastor? I thought I had a cogent understanding of my responsibilities when I graduated from the seminary. Everything was clear then. But now I'm confused!"

The realities of leading a middle-sized congregation greatly challenged Andrew Burke's understanding of pastoral ministry and the perception of his role in the pastoral office. In reality, however, this ordeal *beneficially expanded* his vocational self-awareness! But it would take time for him to value his reimaging of what it means to be a pastor.

ROLE RECOGNITION

The role of the ordained leader in a middle-sized congregation is very significant. The midsize church needs good ministerial leadership! Lyle Schaller observed that the middle-sized church, "to a far greater degree than smaller congregations, often is highly dependent on the competence, compatibility, initiative, and tenure of a creative minister. . . A good match can be remarkably productive. A mismatch can be highly disruptive."[1] Excellent professional leadership is essential to the flourishing of the midsize church. But this leadership takes a different form from that typically observed in both small and large churches.

The word *pastor* originates from the Latin word for *shepherd*. As such it derives from the metaphorical sphere of animal husbandry—the care of sheep. The pastoral role is one comparable to a shepherd. The points of comparison between one who tends to sheep on the Judean hillsides and one who leads people in Christian congregations are numerous. They include the functions of guiding, leading, feeding, nourishing, caring for, seeking after the lost, disciplining, correcting, and protecting. The analogy is used in the Bible—both in the Old and New Testaments—for the leaders of God's people (Num. 27:17; Jer. 23:1–4; Ezek. 34:1–10; Zech. 10:3; Acts 20:28; Eph. 4:11; 1 Peter 5:2). The image is employed to depict the role of servant leaders who tend God's flock, God's church.

It is not surprising, then, that the title has gained a dominant usage in referring to leaders in Christian congregations. As was illustrated by the preceding vignette, many associate this term with leaders of small congregations who give direct pastoral care to the people in that community of faith. But one need not limit the term *pastor* to ministers of small churches. Just as there can be flocks of sheep that vary in size—some small, some large, some medium—so also there are congregations of varying size—small, large, midsize. Even as shepherds tend the flocks of divergent sizes, so also it is legitimate to label as pastors the ordained leaders of

---

1. Schaller, *The Middle-Sized Church*, 104.

congregations of all sizes. Accordingly, this is the dominant title used in this book for the ordained professional leader of a Christian congregation.

No matter what the size of the parish, a pastor attends to certain functions that are inherent to the role. These include feeding the members with the nourishing message of the gospel—preaching and teaching the word of God in season and out of season. The pastor administers baptism and the Lord's Supper according to their institution by Christ. The pastor tends to those who are growing in the faith, both young and old, by catechizing them in the basic truths of the Bible and seeing to their maturation under its formative influence. The pastor reproves the erring and disciplines the unrepentant of the flock. The shepherd seeks after the lost to gather them to the fold. The guardian of the flock protects church members from false teachings and dangerous influences that would lead them away from Christ. And the pastor leads, guiding the congregation in a God-pleasing direction to advance the Lord's mission of redemption, reconciliation, and restoration.

In other words, the pastor attends to the priorities that God has entrusted to the church. In this calling he becomes:

- the agent of God to bear the divine *presence* to people via the means of grace;
- the servant of God to deliver divine *power* to the lives of people through the gospel message, a power that brings new life and new obedience through the indwelling Holy Spirit;
- the instrument of God to advance the divine *plan* of restoring creation by God's grace.

These are priorities that all pastors of every size of congregation are to pursue and practice. Accordingly, these are the priorities that pastors of midsize churches embrace.

PASTORAL MODES

The ways in which these priorities are advanced vary among differing contexts of congregations, including size cultures. The way in which pastoring is conducted in a small church differs from that done in a middle-sized parish. And the way in which one shepherds the flock in a midsize church will vary from the manner performed in a large congregation.

What is common to the role in any of these contexts is that *the pastor sees to it that the priorities of God are carried out in the context of this calling.* In a small church, where the average worship attendance is less than 150 each week, the pastor can attend to these responsibilities directly via regular personal face-to-face contact with all members of the flock. In the middle-sized context the pastor will need to delegate some of that work to other staff, leaders, and volunteers. As such, the ordained leader assumes more of a managerial or supervisory role, without completely abdicating some direct one-on-one pastoral care to individuals. This reality is magnified in the context of a large church where 400 or more worshippers gather each week. In such a case the pastor serves more like a chief executive who sees to the execution of the ministry by other professionals.

The clergy of any size congregation have options regarding the modes used to carry out the pastoral role. A mode is simply a manner of behaving, a way to approach the task. The pastoral modes that are most relevant to the culture of a medium church will now be investigated and applied. Each of these modes should be integrated into pastoral practice in a middle-sized context. They are the modes of minister, manager, and leader. Of these three, the mode of manager is more pronounced in the medium parish than in small and large churches.

In comparing the modes of pastoral behavior in small, midsize, and large churches, various depictions have been presented. For example, Gary McIntosh differentiates between the modes by describing the role of the pastor in a small church as a *lover*, in the medium church as an *administrator*, and in the large church as a *leader*.[2] Herb Miller depicts the distinctions as those of *chaplain* for the small church, *C.O.O. (Chief Operating Officer)* for the midsize church, and *C.E.O. (Chief Executive Officer)* for the large church.[3] These are comparable to the three roles that are examined here: minister, manager, and leader. But the fact is that in any size church the pastor should be able to navigate between all three of these roles, with one dominating his attention. The term *manager* will be used in this book to characterize the role most befitting the pastor in a middle-sized congregation. Nonetheless he must also embody the roles of minister and leader to his people. These three roles are complementary, not mutually exclusive.

It should be noted from the outset of this discussion that when pastors adapt to a more managerial focus, this is not a betrayal of the ministry the Lord has given to them. In fact, it is an embracing of that calling, because God has placed them in the particular context of the midsize church, a context which requires management skills. Indeed, certain New Testament descriptors of the pastoral office emphasize these functions of ministry. For example, the Greek word *episkopos* literally translates as one who oversees—a supervisory role (Acts 20:28, 1 Tim. 3:2; Titus 1:7; 1 Peter 5:2). This certainly involves oversight of the doctrine and practice of the congregation, but it entails more. It indicates that the overseer does not necessarily do all the work of ministry, but sees that it gets done by others. An *episkopos* entrusts responsibility for accomplishing some ministry to other consecrated leaders and supervises their work, seeing that it is done with doctrinal integrity and with practical effectiveness. Furthermore,

---

2. McIntosh, *One Size Doesn't Fit All*, 60.
3. Miller, *Coaching Midsize Congregations toward Positive Change*, 18.

Paul employs a verb translated as *manage* (*proistēmi*) and applies it to the work of the pastor (1 Tim. 5:17, see also 1 Tim. 3:5). Thus the Bible itself affirms the need for pastors to exercise management functions in their ministry, as the context demands. As will be seen, the same can be said of the leadership role.

THE MODE OF MINISTER

The word *minister* originates from Latin and means *servant*. In the New Testament the Greek word commonly used for church leaders is *diakonos*, which also translates as *servant*. Jesus called the leaders in his kingdom to be servants (Luke 22:25–26). The apostles who led the early church in Jerusalem saw to the priority of the "ministry of the word" (Acts 6:4). The Apostle Paul affirmed that he and his fellow church leaders were ministers of a new covenant and of the gospel (2 Cor. 3:6–8; Col. 1:23), and had been entrusted with the ministry of reconciliation (2 Cor. 5:18). It is clear from these passages that the focus of ministry (*what* is served) is the gospel message of God's word, and the target of ministry (*who* is served) is people. Accordingly Christian ministers today are called to serve others with the gospel.

The pastor of the midsize church attends to the primary functions of the pastoral office. These include the responsibilities of preaching God's word, leading the worship services, administering baptism and the Lord's Supper, teaching and providing catechetical instruction, visiting the sick and dying, comforting the grieving, counseling the hurting, exercising loving discipline of members, and seeking after the lost. Some of these functions will be shared with others, but they should not be completely abandoned by the pastor. For example, the expectation that the pastor visit all of the members annually in their contexts of living (homes, workplaces, etc.) is unrealistic in a church averaging over 150 worshippers. But this does not mean that the pastor omits visitation completely.

Clergy who are called to a medium congregation still make visits with the people. But these are more selective and intentional. In life-crisis events, the pastor should be personally present with the members. This includes the obvious occasions of death and tragic loss. It continues in the care of those who grieve. It also can involve occasions such as substance abuse intervention or the ministry of presence during a domestic conflict.

Certainly the pastor will continue to make some visits on members who are hospitalized. This may be shared with a staff worker (such as a deacon, deaconess, or retired visitation pastor) or a volunteer care-giver (such as a lay person trained in the Stephen Ministry® process). The minister may participate in a rotating schedule with other staff or volunteers in the regular visitation of hospitalized members and of homebound members. Nevertheless, the shepherd should have some presence in the lives of members who are hospitalized. The members of the middle-sized church can expect their pastor to visit them in critical occasions of spiritual need.

The same is true regarding the visitation of the homebound. The minister of a midsize congregation may not do *all* the regular (e.g., monthly) visits to homebound members. This can be shared with other staff or lay workers. But each homebound member will be visited by the pastor *periodically*, such as on a quarterly basis.

It is my opinion that the pastor of the midsize church should schedule time to visit members in their homes and workplaces. This enables the minister to observe his members in their everyday life settings. Such visits are not necessarily prompted by any special need of the members, such as illness or grief. They are simply for the purpose of getting to know the members. For example, when I was pastor of a medium-size congregation I devoted Thursday evening to home visitation of members, visiting one household each week.

Finally, the pastor will be present in the wider community to make connections with those who are not members of the church. He will look for opportunities to share the gospel with unbelievers and those who are disconnected from the family of God.

The midsize church may be larger than the small church, but it is by no means too large for the pastor to neglect pastoral care and personal visitation. Most pastors of medium-sized congregations, like Pastor Burke, are devoted to living out these primary pastoral functions of ministry. They are dedicated to doing personal ministry. But there are two other modes that the pastor must claim if he wishes effectively to serve in the size culture of the medium church. The most significant of these is the role of manager.

THE MODE OF MANAGER

As was illustrated in the experience of Pastor Burke, pastors frequently have difficulty transitioning from being chaplains in small churches to becoming managers in midsize parishes. Pastors of small congregations are used to engaging in daily pastoral care contact with members, and regularly to do so with *all* the members of the congregation. They are accustomed to doing hands-on ministry directly with the whole body of the church's membership, and their ministry is characterized as highly relational with these members. Pastors of small congregations oftentimes draw great satisfaction from these regular personal relationship encounters and from providing direct pastoral care to all the members when needed. In this context, the minister relates immediately and intimately with all members and knows virtually everything that is happening in the congregation.

But this changes when one becomes the pastor of a church that averages over 150 worshippers. Now the pastor must cultivate skill in helping others to do ministry in a shared responsibility. Rather than performing all the pastoral care and ministry immediately to parishioners, the pastor entrusts much of the hands-on ministry to others, be they staff, program leaders, or volunteers. The chief minister must now manage others in the accomplishment of ministry responsibilities, seeing to it that ministry gets done while not doing it all directly. In this role of oversight, the pastor will not be intimately aware of *all* the goings-on in the congregation; its complexity and the multitude of activities make that impossible. This oftentimes feels messy, and it can be extremely uncomfortable for those who want to control every detail of congregational operations.

This does not mean that the pastor of a midsize church abdicates doing pastoral care. Such an approach takes this principle to an unhealthy extreme. For a pastor to be divested of all involvement in pastoral care would likely be harmful to the medium congregation and to its ministry. As was affirmed in the previous section, the ordained leader still makes visits with the people, but these are more selective and intentional. The pastor still is called to be a minister, but he integrates this role with that of manager.

Another way of looking at this role distinction is to consider how the pastor spends time. Simply put, the pastor of the medium church spends less time in ongoing interaction with every member of the congregation and spends more time engaging with the program staff and lay leadership. He invests much attention in planning with these leaders to develop and execute high quality programming. As congregations increase in size so does the time and energy devoted by the clergy to the tasks of recruiting qualified candidates to lead ministry programs, equipping and training them in their leadership roles, overseeing them, encouraging them, and assessing their efforts. That is, the pastor of the midsize church must exercise much more of a managerial role than the one who shepherds a small congregation.

The midsize parish that welcomes a new pastor could legitimately claim to be "under new management." And the person who enters that role (especially after having served a small church) can appropriately be said to be entering "into new management." Instead of the pastor directly performing all ministry duties, much of it is done by others under his supervision. For this to happen, a high priority must be given to the equipping, coordinating, and supporting of professional personnel and lay leadership. If this management role is neglected, the programmatic efforts of the church will suffer.

The mode of manager most distinguishes the behavior of the pastor of the midsize church from that of those serving small or large parishes. This is a role that clergy in these congregations should accept and adapt to. Since it is such a fundamental role for these pastors, more needs to be said regarding the matters of management.

What and Whom to Manage
The need for the pastor to manage others arises from the distinctive orientation and organization of the midsize church. The church that averages between 150 and 400 worshippers each week is usually programmatic in

its orientation. Thus, a primary target of management will be the various *programs* of the church (*what* is managed) that, practically speaking, are executed through the management of the *leaders* of these programs (*whom* is managed). The medium church operates as a collection of programmatic groups, including boards, committees, classes, circles, clubs, organizations, and fellowships. As demonstrated in the previous chapter, a typical midsize church consists of twenty to thirty program groups of varying sizes. Some describe this size parish as a multi-celled entity.[4] Thus the pastor must give attention to managing the various cells that constitute the congregation. This means especially focusing on the *leaders*—official and unofficial—of those constituent groups.

The pastor of a small congregation gives direct attention to all the members of the church by encouraging them to exercise their gifts and guiding them in ways to do so. The pastor of a medium congregation, however, focuses primarily on the leaders of groups, equipping them to encourage and direct others in ministry. This also entails coordinating the leaders so that their constituent groups do not work at cross purposes with one another. The ordained leader must facilitate cooperation and communication between the various program groups in the parish, which is the task of management.

How to Manage: Planning

The most important way to accomplish coordination of the congregation's programs is through collaborative planning among program leaders. This happens on several levels.

The first level involves the staff. These professional workers, who may be full-time or part-time employees of the congregation, should meet regularly under the leadership of the pastor to identify shared goals for the church and to assess their accomplishment. A comprehensive strategic plan is developed that serves as a roadmap for the forward movement of the church's mission and that aligns all constituent groups to the advancement of that mission. Each staff member then sees to it that the groups that he oversees work in congruence with the plan. Clergy in middle-sized congregations are wise to devote time to meet with individual staff members in order to assure that they are promoting the shared strategic direction of the church in their areas of responsibility.

The second level of collaborative planning involves unpaid volunteer leaders: the elected or appointed directors of boards and chairpersons of committees in the church. These officers should be encouraged to formulate outcomes for at least one year in advance. Such goals are then shared with the leaders of other constituency groups, often in a gathering such

---

4.   Roy M. Oswald, "How to Minister Effectively in Family, Pastoral, Program, and Corporate Sized Churches," in *Size Transitions in Congregations*, ed. Beth Ann Gaede (Herndon, VA: The Alban Institute, 2001), 39; Miller, *Coaching Midsize Churches toward Positive Change*, 14.

as the church council, to assure that there is no unnecessary duplication of effort and to identify areas for collaboration between groups. These lay leaders identify specific activities, events, and efforts that the boards or committees will undertake to accomplish the outcomes and schedule them on a comprehensive shared church calendar that is constantly updated. This planning map and calendar, when effectively communicated, will prevent conflict between constituency groups. The pastor will invest a significant proportion of time in meeting with key board chairpersons and lay leaders. This is to assure that each board and program is aligned to the congregation's strategic plan and is pursuing the agreed upon goals. It also facilitates coordination of the manifold activities that are sponsored by the groups.

The third level of pastoral management is with the unofficial groups of the congregation that meet somewhat independently and emerge sometimes spontaneously. These groups are more difficult to manage because they may not be part of a formal network in the church nor be officially constituted. This may include home Bible studies, women's gatherings, support groups, fellowship cells, and missional communities. The key is to connect each group's leader with the oversight of the church. For example, the congregation's Minister of Christian Education is informed of the development of a home Bible study involving members, and receives periodic reports about the activities of the group. The staff worker can then provide helpful guidance to the group leader and inform him of events sponsored by the church that may be relevant to the study participants. In the case of groups that use the church facilities and sponsor activities that might conflict with other congregational events, it is especially important that communication and coordination take place.

In the above scenarios, the pastor need not be intimately aware of *all* the goings-on of these constituent groups. Nor should he be directly involved in coordinating them. But he should see to it that *systems* are established that manage these groups and their leaders. He should see that a process is in place that coordinates their activities. This is the role of oversight that the pastor must not neglect. The pastor also should be the catalyst for strategic planning among the staff and official leadership team of the parish. Typically this will not happen automatically within the complex collection of programs of a medium congregation, and so it needs to be proactively promoted and directed by the pastor. This is an essential aspect of managing the midsize church.

It is especially wise for the clergy leader to invest the greatest attention and personal support to the leaders of the programs that are most effective in advancing the strategic priorities of the church. The best way to build up and promote fruitful programs is to make it a priority to encourage and edify the leaders of those programs. Frequently the pastor in his role as manager will devote the lion's share of attention to program leaders who are struggling or even failing. No doubt these individuals need some attention, but this should not be to the neglect of those leaders who are functioning effectively. The clergy leader should primarily invest in program leaders who are productive.

In carrying out his role as manager, the pastor undertakes to strengthen the effective functioning of the leaders of the important constituency groups in the church, especially if these leaders are professional staff or elected board chairpersons. Subsequent chapters will address the development of these leaders—both paid staff and volunteers.

Management Span

Another important dynamic about management in the middle-sized church has to do with the scope or span of that management. The pastor is to attend to not only *whom* he manages, but also *how many* others he manages.

Because pastors are finite creatures, their capacity to manage others is also finite. In other words, there is a limit to how many staff, lay leaders, or volunteers any given pastor can effectively manage. Some clergy are more gifted in management and will be able to oversee a higher number of workers. Others will have the capacity to manage fewer people. But there is a breaking point for each of us, and we need to be aware of this and not overextend ourselves in responsibility. This is called *span of control*, and it refers to the number of people or program areas that one person can manage. Kevin Martin maintains that a managing pastor's span of control should never extend into double digits. He observes that "if a pastor is directly responsible for managing more than nine areas at once, the areas begin to manage the pastor."[5]

An organization manifests a wide span of control when a manager has relatively many people—usually five to ten—who are directly accountable to him. This organizational structure is illustrated in the following diagram:

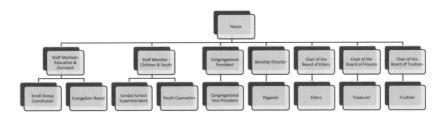

Note that in this example the pastor directly oversees seven other people. The greater number of people to supervise creates a wider breadth of management.

---

5.   Martin, *The Myth of the 200 Barrier*, 82.

A narrow span of control exists when the manager has only a few—usually two to four—workers who directly report to him. This organizational structure is diagrammed as follows:

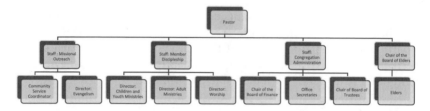

Note that in this example the pastor directly oversees only four other people. This diagram demonstrates that a narrow span of control involves fewer direct accountability relationships that the pastor must manage. So relative to the responsibilities for management it is narrower.

Most midsize congregations demonstrate organizational charts with a wide span of control, whereas in most large churches the organizational chart is narrow. Generally speaking, the larger the congregation the narrower the span of control. This is because in a large church the ministry operations are much more professionalized, so that the head pastor primarily oversees other professional staff who are well trained (and well paid) and who are highly accountable for their work. However, in the middle-sized church the staff team is usually small (i.e., involving one to three paid workers in addition to the pastor) and is typically less professionalized (e.g., promoted from being volunteers). This requires more direct supervision of each staff worker by the pastor. Supplemented to this is the need for the pastor's direct supervision of prominent lay leaders. Finally, the multi-cell structure and program-oriented nature of the midsize church functions best if there remains one central manager—the pastor—to whom most of the program leaders report. This organizational structure is therefore relatively flat and involves few layers of management.

The wide span of control model involving the singular central manager has several advantages: coordination is centralized, communication is more streamlined, and expenses are minimized (since there are fewer professional managers on the payroll). The challenge, of course, rests solidly with the central manager—the pastor—who must oversee several workers and be accessible to almost every program leader. The strain of managing all these relationships can be great, and this is one of the most significant burdens that pastors of medium churches bear.

Sometimes the pastor is not able to handle this managerial burden, and other options must be considered. One alternative is to bring onto the staff an executive manager who is not ordained to assume much of the administrative load. But rarely is this financially feasible for midsize congregations. This is why in most cases pastors of midsize churches must cultivate skills in managing others. Nonetheless, it is also wise for pastors to set *boundaries* on management. The principle cited earlier is a wise one to implement—the pastor's span of control should be limited to single digits—no more than nine staff or program leaders to be directly managed.

THE MODE OF LEADER

This chapter has emphasized that the pastor of a medium church must behave as a manager. That mode is vitally important to the effective functioning of the midsize congregation. On the one hand, the typical small church requires pastoral presence that can be characterized as chaplaincy. On the other hand, the large church benefits from a head pastor who operates as an executive. Between these two size cultures is the middle-sized church. Its distinctive characteristics and culture usually necessitate that the pastor assumes a role that is highly managerial.

As has been already argued, this does not mean that clergy in medium congregations operate in a manner that is devoid of traditional ministry skills. They continue to function in the mode of minister, exercising caregiving functions that are valued in the small church. Yet also at the other end of the skill spectrum, the effective minister of the midsize church is not without executive leadership skills that are especially valued in pastors of the large church.

Social scientists and organizational theorists frequently distinguish between management and leadership.[6] According to this distinction a leader focuses on strategic issues (e.g., visioning, long-range planning, conceptualizing outcomes by working from the future to the present) while a manager gives attention to the operational matters of the organization (e.g., implementing the vision, mobilizing resources, and conceptualizing plans by working from the present to the future). The leader articulates the strategic direction while the manager aligns workers to that destination and organizes them to achieve it. The leader is more initiating—being concerned with innovation and exploration—whereas the manager is more maintaining—showing concern for procedures and processes.

It is in light of these distinctions between management and leadership that we qualify the role of pastors serving medium-sized churches. Although much of their behavior will correspond to the functions described as managerial, they also should give attention to those behaviors that demonstrate leadership. Clergy in midsize parishes must be strategically oriented as well as operationally savvy. They demonstrate the attributes of leadership such as being visionary, adventurous, and innovative.

---

6. For example, see John P. Kotter, *Leading Change* (Boston, MA: Harvard Business Review Press, 2012), 28–33; and Peter G. Northouse, *Leadership: Theory and Practice*, 5th ed. (Los Angeles: SAGE Publications, 2010), 9–11.

They will pioneer new ventures for the congregation and will guide the members to journey with them.

One peril that often besets pastors of medium churches is that they become so operationally oriented that they neglect the task of leading. The time and effort invested in managing the many programs of the medium congregation are so consuming that little energy is left to think and act strategically for the future of the congregation. The varied operations of the church may function efficiently and smoothly, but this homeostasis may cause the pastor to be satisfied only with the status quo.

Leadership, however, involves much more than that! Pastors must also catalyze change. They must show courage to venture into paths yet untrodden and to enlist others to follow. Ultimately, the pastor must guide the congregation to advance the distinctive mission that God has entrusted to it. This means to oppose inertia and to empower others so that they move forward in accomplishing God's purposes and priorities in an ever-changing world.

There is a great need for strategic leadership in midsize churches, and pastors are the ones most responsible to provide it. But they need not do so alone; indeed, they *must* not do it alone. This is where the multi-cell and programmatic nature of the medium church comes to bear. Leadership originates in the constituency groups and the most important decisions are made by the prominent figures in those groups. As Gary McIntosh observes, change in the medium church is initiated from the *middle-out* through key committees and programs. This contrasts with the process of change in a small church, which is *bottom-up* (originating from key family leaders such as the congregational patriarch or matriarch). It also differs from the large church, in which change is initiated from the *top-down*, that is, by the senior pastor who influences staff and those who sit on the governing board of the church.[7]

Thus pastoral leadership in the midsize parish does not require the pastor to assume an authoritarian role, unilaterally setting the vision and then barking out orders to get it done. That is a recipe for pastor disaster! Instead, initiatives for new directions in the church are determined jointly with the congregation's lay leadership group and the key figures in the various programs and constituency groups. The accomplishment of the vision depends highly upon how that vision originated and who owns it. In the middle-size congregation the origination of most innovation occurs in the programmatic groups and its ownership must also be by those groups. Thus in exercising effective leadership, the pastor will work collaboratively and collegially with the leaders of those groups. The old adage, *change imposed is change opposed*, applies to the culture of midsize congregations. But when pastors work together with other key leaders, positive transformation can happen.

---

7. McIntosh, *One Size Doesn't Fit All*, 98–100.

Pastoral leadership can also involve speaking contrary to the prevailing opinion. When working collaboratively with key stakeholders, there is the need for a prophetic voice. Oftentimes the pastor must be a catalyst for reformation. The natural disposition of congregational members, including program directors, is to maintain the status quo. The unspoken mantra is this: "Come weal or woe, my status is quo!" Thus the pastor must challenge others to think in new ways and to pursue new opportunities. Sometimes this means to question established patterns of behavior and even to denounce these when they are contrary to the priorities of God. This takes courage and tact. The capable clergy leader demonstrates genuine appreciation for the heritage of the congregation and values its worthwhile traditions, while patiently guiding its most influential members to adjust ministry methods to meet the challenges of changing times. All the while the pastor will hold the best interests of the corporate church in mind and a deep love for each member in his heart.

Therefore, the pastor of the middle-sized parish will integrate the skills of leadership and management. It is not a matter of either-or, but of both-and. Because of the dynamics distinctive to the size culture of this congregation, the managerial role will usually dominate in the performance of the pastor's responsibilities. But this is never to the exclusion of the functions that typify true leadership. The shepherd guides the flock into new ventures while always seeing to its security and safety.

THE INTERSECTION OF MINISTRY, MANAGEMENT, AND LEADERSHIP

Many ordained leaders perceive that to assume more of an administrative role—functioning in the modes of manager and leader—is to abandon an interpersonal focus in ministry and therefore to neglect true ministry. When this happened to Pastor Burke he assumed that he had abdicated his pastoral responsibilities. It can seem less personal and more bureaucratic to shift one's priorities to activities involved in planning, delegating, coordinating, training, supervising, and evaluating. Frequently pastors who assume this role are dissatisfied and even feel guilty.

Although it is certainly possible that a manager or executive leader can be impersonal and bureaucratic, this need not be the case. Indeed, the best administrators are those who are highly personal and excel in interpersonal relationships. The difference is that the personal relationships the pastor cultivates as a manager or leader are concentrated not upon each individual member of the congregation but on key personnel—professional staff, program coordinators, and lay officers. "When clergy move from a pastoral- to program-size church," Roy Oswald observes, "they will experience tension and difficulty in their new congregation unless they are ready to shift from a primarily interpersonal mode to a program planning and development mode. It is not that clergy will have no further need for their interpersonal skills. Far from it—they will depend on them even more. But now those interpersonal skills will be placed at the service of the parish program."[8]

It is incumbent upon the one who accepts a call to shepherd a midsize church to come to terms with this reality. The pastor must make peace with the idea that management is a form of ministry. The two are not mutually exclusive practices, but rather are integrated. Louis Weeks, in a book aptly entitled *All for God's Glory: Redeeming Church Scutwork*, affirms this integration of church management and pastoral ministry in contending that "good planning makes for excellent worship and nurture; mission and witness are inextricable from effective organization; deep, trusting partnership among pastor, staff, and lay leadership are built on keeping promises and meeting responsibilities."[9] Simply stated, the effectiveness of a midsize church's *ministry* and *mission* is highly dependent on effective *management* and *leadership*. In the typical midsize church, no one is more responsible for management and leadership than the ordained clergy leader.

If the pastor can function only as a chaplain to the members and is not able to develop management and leadership skills, then the midsize church will most likely decline in membership, eventually becoming a small parish where this style of pastoral ministry is appropriate. Put otherwise, if the style of ministry provided by the pastor will not conform to the size culture of the congregation, that size culture is likely to conform eventually to the style of ministry of the clergy leader.

If the pastor is unwilling or unable to adjust his style of ministry to fit the size culture of a medium church, he may acknowledge this misalignment and leave the midsize congregation in order to serve a small one. A second option is for the pastor to remain in the medium church and attend to the chaplaincy needs of its members while another professional leader is brought to the staff to focus on the administrative responsibilities in that church. "It is possible for pastors who are strong caregivers to lead middle-sized churches," Gary McIntosh notes, "but they will need to share leadership with an administrative assistant or an assistant pastor who will handle the bulk of administrative details."[10]

In any case, for a medium church to continue to survive—and especially to thrive—the programmatic nature of its size culture must be respected and cultivated. That means that ministry must be provided that is administrative in nature. At least one of the primary leaders of a midsize church must be a gifted manager, and that role usually falls to the

---

8. Oswald, "How to Ministry Effectively in Family, Pastoral, Program, and Corporate Sized Churches," 40.

9. Louis B. Weeks, *All for God's Glory: Redeeming Church Scutwork* (Herndon, VA: The Alban Institute, 2008), 6.

10. McIntosh, *Taking Your Church to the Next Level*, 147.

pastor. If he has executive leadership skills, all the better! All the while he attends to the primary tasks of ministry in the congregation, which include preaching, worship leadership, teaching, pastoral care, and visitation. The pastor of the midsize church is called to integrate the modes of ministry, management, and leadership.

This is the challenge of being a pastor of a midsize congregation. It is daunting indeed, and may seem overwhelming at times. But none of us can shepherd the flock apart from the grace given by the Chief Shepherd. Jesus Christ is the one who calls frail vessels to the office of pastor and fills them with his Spirit in order to be competent for the task. He gives courage to lead and wisdom to manage well. He also gives grace to the weak when they flounder and fail. God does not leave pastors to fare on their own, but he provides his life-giving presence and life-changing power to equip them to shepherd his flock.

SUMMARY

The core functions of pastoral ministry are consistent no matter what is the size of a congregation. Its priorities remain constant—bearing God's gracious presence, delivering God's generative power, and advancing God's redemptive plan. Nevertheless, sociological and organizational dynamics related to the sheer number of people in the congregational system influence the pastor's approach to serve the flock effectively. The distinctive dynamics of a midsize congregation require the pastor to adjust his pastoral modes to be most effective. He attends to three significant modes.

The first mode is that of *ministry* itself. The pastor assumes the role of a servant. He is a servant for God and to the people. He is a servant of the word and of the gospel. He sees to the delivery of God's means of grace through preaching, leading worship, administering baptism and the Lord's Supper, teaching, visiting members, caregiving, and seeking the lost. Some of this the pastor does directly and personally. In other cases he sees to the execution of this ministry by others. But he dare not neglect the ministerial role that has been entrusted to him.

The second pastoral mode in the midsize congregation is that of *manager*. In the programmatic system that is typical of the medium parish, the pastor's role becomes highly managerial. The person who is called to shepherd a middle-sized church must learn to be a manager of the various constituency groups which compose the congregation. In adapting to this role, it should be remembered that equipping and enabling others to do ministry is itself ministry. Pastors of middle-sized congregations who are engaged in administration and management functions may feel that they are neglecting the ministry to which they are called. But in actuality they are multiplying ministry by empowering others to serve.

Finally, the pastor of a midsize congregation is to function as a *leader*. This is the third pastoral mode which clergy are to embody. He sees to it that not only do the programs of the parish run smoothly, but these are moving forward toward the accomplishment of God's purposes and priorities for the church. As such, pastors will act courageously to advance the mission of God in their midst.

The underlying assumption is that the modes of ministry, management, and leadership involve engagement with people. These entail relationships with others. This is good news! For God also sends other people—co-workers—to assist the pastor and to share the responsibilities of ministry (1 Cor. 3:9). Granted, these are people whom the pastor manages and leads. But they are also partners in the mission and ministry entrusted to the church. The following chapters provide guidance as to how this vital participation of professional staff and lay volunteers can be maximized so that the midsize congregation is mobilized to participate in God's mission and to pursue God's priorities.

CHAPTER 8

PERSONNEL

Andrew Burke believed that it was time for a second full-time position to be added to the program staff of Faith Church. This would be a milestone because in the history of the congregation there had only been one full-time paid professional position. That was the post that he now filled—the pastor. As the church had grown, staff positions were developed to attend to the burgeoning needs of the congregation: a Director of Music Ministry, a Youth Director, and a Service Gifts Coordinator. But these positions were part-time; the workers were contracted for no more than fifteen hours a week each. Moreover, the Youth Director had recently taken a position in another city and moved away. So that position needed to be filled.

Pastor Burke also believed that one critical area of the church's ministry, Christian education, had not achieved its potential to form the faith of children and adults at Faith Church. The quality of the Sunday school program was mediocre, and the number of children participating was diminishing. Although he loved to teach Bible studies and adult education courses, Pastor Burke realized that being the sole teacher in these areas was severely limiting the potential for members to be taught the faith. Others should share in this teaching role, but they would need to be recruited, equipped, and supervised. And Andrew didn't wish to add one more area of management to his list of responsibilities. He also was convinced that a system of small groups should be developed through which the members of Faith Church, especially the newcomers, could find a community of belonging and study. But he didn't have the time or motivation to lead this initiative. These were primary reasons for adding another staff position.

Furthermore, it became increasingly clear that the responsibilities of several critical programs had become too challenging to be handled by any lay volunteer, or even by a paid part-time lay worker. In earlier years the education program of the congregation had been a responsibility shared between the pastor and the Board of Christian Education. The pastor taught several classes such as Bible studies, junior confirmation instruction, and the adult information class for inquirers seeking membership in the church. The Board of

Christian Education developed and coordinated the Sunday school program, and the Sunday morning education classes for teens and adults. Similarly, the congregation's program for young people—teenagers in the congregation—was administered by the part-time Director of Youth with assistance from members of the Board of Youth Ministry. This included regular Sunday evening gatherings—held on the first and third Sundays for senior high students and on the second and fourth Sundays for junior high youth. The Director of Youth had oversight of semi-annual youth retreats (again split evenly between the high school and junior high groups) and a shared annual servant event in the summer. But now she had moved to another city.

It was evident to the leaders of these boards, and to an increasingly overwhelmed pastor, that the work in these areas was too much for volunteers to handle. The congregation now had reached a Sunday worship attendance average of over 275. The remaining part-time staff positions—the Service Gifts Coordinator and the Director of Music Ministry—were compensated for a total of thirty hours per week. This was significantly less than the equivalent of one full time worker (FTE). The fact that the congregation had reached this size indicated that it was due for the addition of another staff position, only in this case not another part-time position but a full time one. It was time for the church to take the next step. So Pastor Burke developed a proposal to establish a new staff position to take on these pressing needs. The result was the establishment of the position of Director of Education and Youth. A job description was formulated and a search committee was formed to identify candidates for the position.

PERSONNEL PRESSURES

It is inevitable that a middle-sized congregation will need to employ personnel to form a multiple staff. Herb Miller asserts that by definition medium congregations are multiple-staff entities.[1] That is not the case with most small churches. Arlin Routhauge labeled the small church of 50 to 150 (average worship attendance) as the *pastoral* church because it can be adequately served by one pastor who is the central figure of the operations of the parish. A distinctive characteristic of the small church is that the members have their spiritual needs met directly by the pastor. Most, if not all, of the official events and meetings of the congregation involve the attendance of the pastor. This is manageable for the pastor to handle, because the demands are not too great for one person.

But when a congregation passes the threshold of 150 active worshippers, its clergy leader becomes stretched. It becomes impossible for one person to deliver direct one-on-one attention to every spiritual concern of all the congregation's members. As noted in the previous chapter, the

---

1.   Herb Miller, *Coaching Midsize Congregations toward Positive Change*, 13.

pastor of the midsize parish must transition from doing direct ministry with people to the work of managing others to do ministry.

Regularly those others are staff members who are employed by the congregation and compensated financially for their services. The actual roles and titles of these staff members vary from context to context. Frequently the staff associates will oversee ministry areas such as youth and education, as was the case with the position developed at Faith Church. Other ministry functions commonly attended to by program staff are outreach, worship, family ministry, and discipleship.

Sometimes a staff person will focus only on one ministry area, but in a midsize church that usually occurs when the worker is employed part-time, not full time. In the case of someone employed full-time by the medium church, the usual expectation is that she will oversee multiple areas of ministry.

This chapter on personnel acquisition addresses the pressures to add program staff. It offers a process for doing so effectively with maximal results. Regularly the medium church will be led by a pastor who collaborates with several coworkers in the employment of the congregation. What follows is a presentation of a process for securing these additional paid staff workers who support the chief shepherd in feeding and leading the flock.

ADDING STAFF

Citing data from the National Congregations Study, Alice Mann reports that two-thirds of midsize congregations operate with three or less full-time paid staff. One-third of medium parishes function with more than three full-time staff workers. Accordingly, the staff system of the typical midsize church is not large, usually only two to four full-time workers. Mann also reports that about forty percent of middle-sized parishes use additional part-time workers as staff members.[2]

This data indicates that eventually congregations of this size will need to add staff. How do congregational leaders proceed in the quest to add staff? I recommend they do so by asking and answering five fundamental questions: why, what, when, where, and who. Answering the question of *how* is assumed in this process, since the overarching question being addressed is this: How do congregational leaders proceed in searching to add staff?

WHY? ARTICULATING THE NEED

The first question congregational leaders should ask is *why*, or more specifically, "Why do we need an additional staff member?" In other words, what is the reason for adding staff? Leaders of midsize churches will do well to articulate the purpose of a new staff position before looking for a person to fill the position.

---

2. Mann, *Raising the Roof*, 9.

There are various reasons for securing additional program staff. One reason is to relieve the pastor and other workers (staff and lay) from being over-burdened in their workload. This is especially true of a congregation that is transitioning from being pastor-centered (a small church) to being program-centered (a middle-sized church). Such a congregation will be constrained to add a program staff worker in order to relieve the sole pastor of burgeoning obligations that accompany this change in the congregation's size culture. But also within the size range of the medium church, 150 to 400 average worshippers, the demands upon the professional staff will increase exponentially as the church grows. Timothy Keller observes that as a church grows, so does its complexity: "There is more diversity in factors such as age, family status, ethnicity, and so on, and thus a church of 400 needs four to five times more programs than a church of 200—not two times more."[3] This increased demand for programs requires increased staffing for those programs, which increases the workload of existing staff. Thus adding staff can relieve the burden of a heavy workload currently being borne by workers.

As just noted, the demand for programs, a demand that typifies the midsize church, requires staffing for the programs. This leads to the second reason for adding staff. The staff workers often become the ones who make the programs work. In order for a program to thrive, its operations must be overseen by someone. Somebody must spearhead the effort and be responsible for its execution.

It is possible that lay volunteers can effectively lead programs. However, the dynamics of a midsize church will generally call for more than unpaid volunteers to direct programs. Because of increased complexity in the system, expanded specialization of efforts, and expectations of higher quality in programming, there arises the need for professional leadership of the programs, or at least semi-professional involvement (i.e., part-time paid staff). Volunteers typically lead programs for only a brief period of time—say for a year or two.

In the mid-size church the need develops for greater continuity and thus for more permanent leadership. This often can be attained only by hiring paid staff to oversee the programs. A characteristic of many volunteer-led programs is inconsistency in the quality of those programs. Participants in the programs offered by the middle-size parish expect consistency and a much higher level of quality than what is acceptable in a small church. Paid professional or semi-professional staff can be held accountable to see that this higher standard of quality is achieved and maintained.

The focus of the staff's efforts should not only be to provide ministry and care to the congregation's members, as important as that is. The efforts of staff workers, and the focus of the programs they oversee, should also be directed to those outside of the church. Accordingly, the addition of staff should always have this outreach outcome in mind. Members must

---

3. Keller, *Leadership and Church Size Dynamics*, 3.

constantly be reminded that the primary purpose of the Christian church, and of its individual congregations and members, is to deliver the word of the gospel to others. This is the divine plan for us: to bring the word of God's judgment of sin and his redemption in Christ to all who do not yet know or believe it. Staff workers should be committed to this outreach, and be released and resourced by the congregation to do so.

A couple of final observations regard the question of *why* to add staff. First, an inappropriate response is to hire professional workers so that the members who are unpaid are relieved of their responsibility to serve. Staff workers are not meant to *replace* lay workers; they are meant to *engage* the laity. Parishes that add staff workers who recognize this goal and are intentional to accomplish it have the potential to experience a virtual explosion of lay participation in ministry. Involvement by members is multiplied, not diminished. For example, a congregation at which I was a pastor added a position of Cantor (the Director of Worship and Music). Some members assumed that this staff person would perform most of the church's music single-handedly. However, the cantor understood that his primary role was to enlist and engage the musical talents of others. Within one year of beginning this position, the cantor had recruited and involved over seventy-five members and non-members in the congregation's music ministry. Rather than monopolizing ministry, effective staff workers multiply ministry by maximizing the use of the gifts that God has entrusted to the congregation's members.

A second observation is that staffing frequently comes before programming. In other words, the process is not first the establishment of a program and then the selection of a staff person to coordinate it, but rather the other way around. The staff person is secured because the congregation sees a need for programming that is not yet developed. Then the paid worker becomes the catalyst to this programmatic emphasis. Gary McIntosh observes that declining or plateaued churches frequently place their priorities in this order: facilities, programs, staff. McIntosh maintains that this order should be reversed, making the recruitment and development of effective staff the top priority, with programming next and the provision of facilities last. This prioritization is more conducive to growth and innovation.[4] The addition of staff should extend the congregation's reach into new demographic contexts and relational networks. New program personnel should multiply the impact of the church's mission by engaging more participants (from both inside and outside the church's membership).

WHAT? DEFINING A POSITION

Once the ministry need has been articulated and the case made for adding a staff position, that position must be defined. What will the position look

---

4.   McIntosh, *One Size Doesn't Fit All*, 95.

like? What responsibilities will it entail? Congregational leaders do well to answer these questions and clarify what the new staff person's roles are. This will facilitate a shared understanding about what is expected from the person who fills this position. Everyone—the supervising pastor, the congregational leaders, the congregational members, and the candidates for the position—must be on the same page regarding the expectations for the position.

Components of the Position Description

The process of defining a staff position should result in a written ministry position document. This serves as a covenant between the congregation and the called or contracted worker. It is an important instrument of clarity, communication, and accountability. This job description document benefits the congregation because it is the means to assess how well the staff worker attends to her responsibilities and is meeting stated expectations. It benefits the employed worker because she has clear direction in terms of what is expected of her.

One of the most common problems in multi-staff ministry is that employed staff workers view their primary responsibilities differently than do their supervising pastor or the congregational members. Without a written ministry position description that is approved by the congregational leadership, there will arise a divergent variety of expectations for the staff worker with no means of arbitrating whose expectations have priority. This inevitably leads to some congregational leaders and members becoming dissatisfied with the employed worker. It also leads to a high level of frustration for the staff person. This scenario has the potential to develop into significant conflict among the parties involved. Thus it is wise to head off problems and lay the groundwork for success early in the process by formulating a ministry position description. From the start expectations need to be clear, and a ministry position description is a tool to accomplish this.

The ministry position description document should be comprised of three basic components: responsibilities, qualifications, and accountability.

Responsibilities: The program areas the staff person will supervise are defined, and under each of these broad areas of responsibility are identified more specific duties. Any given job description for a full-time staff person should contain no more than eight major responsibilities. This should not be at the level of detailed specific operational tasks but should express broader strategic duties, giving the worker freedom to function creatively within certain boundaries of responsibility.

Qualifications: This section identifies what personal qualities are needed to carry out the role. These qualities include skills and abilities to achieve the responsibilities. The ministry position may require a specific academic degree or certificate. The description document may articulate what level of field experience is expected for the position. Ecclesial positions often will require adherence to a confession of faith and conformity to moral and ethical standards. Denominations may distinguish between called and commissioned workers. This list of qualifications provides a baseline for the characteristics that are expected of the worker.

Accountability: This section identifies to whom the staff worker is accountable. It clarifies to whom the worker is to report and by whom her work is evaluated. A clear line of accountability is drawn to the person (e.g., lead pastor, board chairperson) or body (e.g., the elders' board, personnel committee) that assesses the effectiveness of the staff worker's labors.

CONFIGURATION OF THE POSITION

In defining the new staff position—that is, identifying *what* it will be—a decision should be made regarding its configuration as a full time or part time position. This defines how the workload is configured regarding how many hours per week are expected of the worker.

Frequently the assumption is made that if a new program staff position is added, it will involve a full time employee. But this need not be the case. If it is the approach, it is helpful to identify what is the expectation for the number of hours spent in this work during a typical week. Is it forty hours? Is it more than that? The reality is that most full time ministry positions, just as with most professional careers, involve the expectation that the worker will invest more than forty hours of labor in the role each week. I think that fifty hours on average is reasonable, recognizing that some seasons will be more demanding than others. This should be clearly articulated so that everyone is in agreement regarding the staff worker's expected investment of time.

There are several advantages to employing full time professional staff. First is that the worker typically has been well trained and equipped for the tasks assigned to her before assuming the position. Frequently she will have been formed for ministry in an educational institution such as a Bible college, Christian university, or theological seminary. She likely will have received significant theological instruction that equips her to carry out ministry in a doctrinally sound manner and with familiarity with best practices.

The second advantage is that the full time church worker will likely provide consistent quality that exceeds what might be offered by several volunteers and even exceeds that performed by part-time staff. The third benefit is one of permanence. Volunteers come and go, and part-time workers stay at the task as long as it doesn't compete with other obligations and sources of income. But full-time workers have consecrated themselves to this calling and are dependent upon the position for their livelihood. Accordingly, they are more inclined to remain committed to the task even when the going gets tough.

But this does not mean that there is no place for part-time staff in a congregation. Indeed, frequently this is a very wise option. There are several good reasons to consider utilizing paid staff workers on a half-time or part-time basis.

First, if the congregational membership is indisposed to add a full-time staff member, especially if finances are limited, employing part-time staff may be a resourceful way to ease into the concept of multiplying staff. This becomes a practical way to make the transition from volunteer leadership to paid directorship of a program. It can ease reluctant parishioners to the idea of having additional paid staff by diminishing the financial risk.

Second, frequently these semi-professional positions can be filled with candidates who are raised up within the congregation. More will be said of this later, but suffice it to say now that such homegrown staff workers are often readily available and have a proven track record. Because they already are established in the congregation and community, there is less risk of a bad fit. Part-time employment is also less of an economic problem both for the congregation and for the staff worker, since the latter usually has other sources for her personal livelihood.

A third advantage of employing part-time paid staff is that it can lead to greater economy. Put crassly, the congregation frequently gets more bang for the buck from this arrangement. In his study of midsize churches, Herb Miller compared part-time lay staff specialists with full-time professional generalists and concluded that the accomplishments of the part-time workers is greater per dollar spent.[5] Churches having employed part-time staff typically report that multiple part-time positions produce up to fifty percent more results for the same expense compared to a single full-time professional with comparable responsibilities. This is especially the case when those filling part-time positions do not receive benefits such as health insurance and a retirement pension from the church.[6]

A fourth advantage of using part-time staff is that the worker is able to focus on areas of personal competence and passion. Assuming that the position requires specialization, a part-time employee can be hired who will focus directly on that effort and who has demonstrated the ability to produce desired results in that area. That is, when a congregation calls or hires a full-time professional with disparate responsibilities, it is likely that this individual will excel at some of those responsibilities but be less effective at others. In the case of part-time employees, the congregation plays to their strengths, and pays for them, without having to tolerate weaknesses.

There are, however, some potential disadvantages to employing part-time staff. One challenge is that part-time personnel are more difficult to supervise. This is particularly true of homegrown staff, but it is also true of semiprofessionals who are brought in from the outside. The reality is that

---

5. Miller, *Coaching Midsize Congregations toward Positive Change*, 13.

6. This raises an ethical issue. A Christian congregation should not neglect the creaturely needs of its workers, and that includes health care and provision for retirement. If these needs are being covered from other sources, such as a spouse's benefit package, then the congregation may be freed from providing such benefits. Congregations must avoid any form of exploitation of their workers. Note the ethical exhortations of Leviticus 19:13, Deuteronomy 24:14–15, Matthew 10:10, Luke 10:7, 1 Corinthians 9:14, and 1 Timothy 5:18.

part-time employees have obligations other than those assigned by the church. They have other commitments that demand their attention (such as to other employers and to family responsibilities). This can contribute to inconsistency in the quality of their work.

Another potential problem is the issue of permanence, since employees may view the part-time responsibility as an extra-curricular activity of a lesser priority to other opportunities in life. This makes supervision more difficult, since accountability can be perceived as being more tenuous.

These are all issues that should be considered when adding staff in a midsize church. The matter of the configuration of these positions— whether full-time or part-time—is significant when identifying *what* the staff position will look like. The ministry description statement should articulate this matter clearly along with identifying the responsibilities, qualifications, and line of accountability for the position.

WHEN? CONFIRMING THE TIMING

How do pastors and other church leaders know when it is time to add staff to the ministry team? When is it appropriate and even necessary to do so? These are important questions to ask and answer. As with the previously addressed questions of *why* and *what*, there is no invariable prescription for all situations and contexts. But some general principles exist that inform a wise decision to add staff at a given time in the history of a medium-sized congregation.

Need Impacts the Timing
The first issue to consider regarding when to add staff has to do with need. Is the new position needed? If so, how badly? The greater the urgency to fill a ministry need, the greater the internal motivation will be to do so.

However, this dynamic should be nuanced. A healthy church should not just react to a long existent urgent need. It should be proactive in anticipating that need before it becomes excessively urgent and ministry opportunities have been neglected. Ordinarily a church should staff beyond its current needs in order to keep growing. In other words, the healthy congregation will stay ahead of the curve and will proactively staff to grow rather than reacting to meet urgent needs. A balance should be at play here: the church adds staff to address existing needs, but it also staffs to engage emerging opportunities for mission and ministry.

Sometimes the need is to replace volunteers with employees. A scenario might look like this. A mission effort or ministry program is critical to the well-being of the congregation. It has been led by a volunteer worker who has become overwhelmed with the responsibilities. Perhaps there is a growing need for consistent quality and accountability that cannot be realized with volunteer leadership. It becomes clear that the oversight of a church's program has become more complex than a lay volunteer can provide. Accordingly, the congregation will seek to staff that position with one who has professional training and expertise. These are valid occasions to consider transitioning from leadership by volunteers to oversight by paid staff.

Size Impacts the Timing

There are also size dynamics that impact the decision of when to add staff. A common practice of congregational consultants is to identify a standard ratio of program staff to average worship attendance. That is, church size—as measured by average worship attendance—can be a valid indicator of the need to add staff. Although each congregation is distinctive and no cookie cutter prescriptions can be made, in general the identification of a standard ratio has value in identifying the appropriate time to add staff.

Lyle Schaller was one of the first to use average weekend worship attendance as a guideline for staffing a church. In 1980 he proposed a ratio of one full time program staff position to a hundred weekend worshippers (1:100) as the standard for most Protestant congregations.[7] This equation was affirmed by Roy Oswald in 1992.[8]

This has proven functionally untenable for many congregations, however, because they cannot afford the financial challenge of staffing at a ratio of 1:100. Gary McIntosh advocates that a ratio of one professional staff position for every 150 worshippers (1:150) is more realistic, basing this on averages from records in the *Yearbook of American and Canadian Churches* from 1915 to 1980.[9] McIntosh applies this ratio to the issue of congregational growth. He advises that "the 1:150 ratio means a church desiring to grow to the next level should add a new staff person *before* reaching the projected growth level. . . . It is the addition of the next staff person that helps a church grow to the next level. The congregation averaging 150 to 175 in worship attendance should be in the process of adding a second person to the program staff if the leaders expect their congregation to grow to 300 worshippers and to be able to assimilate new persons into the life of the church."[10]

A church usually doesn't call its first pastor when it reaches an average attendance of 150. It has done so much earlier. Instead, according to this plan the second pastor or program staff person is added at the 150 attendance level, the third at the 300 level, the fourth at the 450 level, and so on.[11] It should be noted that these figures assume full-time equivalent positions, but the addition of staff can be made more incrementally using part-time workers.[12]

---

7.   Lyle Schaller, *The Multiple Staff and the Larger Church* (Nashville: Abingdon, 1980), 59.

8.   Roy Oswald, *Making Your Church More Inviting* (Herndon, VA: The Alban Institute, 1992), 16.

9.   McIntosh, *Staff Your Church for Growth*, 39–40.

10. Ibid., 41–42.

11. McIntosh, *One Size Doesn't Fit All,* 93.

12. One FTE equates to two half-time staff members, four quarter-time staff members, or other equivalent combinations.

Nevertheless, there is still support for Lyle Schaller's original proposal of a ratio of 1:100. Gary McIntosh himself seems to prefer this as the best possible scenario in recommending that a midsize church aspire to the ratios (FTE staff to worship attendance) of 2:200 and 3:300. He maintains that "by adding the third pastoral staff person at this point, the church will have the best chance of moving beyond the four hundred attendance barrier. Following this hiring pattern throughout the life of the church will ensure that the ministry has an excellent chance of expansion."[13]

Herb Miller advocates for a similar approach. In counsel specifically directed to midsize churches, he states that the threshold for adding a second FTE staff member is at 150 average worshippers, but thereafter FTE staff workers are to be added at intervals of one hundred (i.e., two FTE at 150, three at 250, four at 350, five at 450, etc.).[14]

It is appropriate, therefore, that congregational leaders use these admittedly varying guidelines with discernment, factoring in other considerations such as the systemic complexity of the church. Every congregation is unique and will need to determine the appropriate time to add staff. Nonetheless, for the typical midsize church a reasonable ratio of FTE pastoral/program staff to average weekend worship attendance is between 1:100 and 1:150.

Resources Impact the Timing

Of course, staffing is dependent upon financial resources. Compensating professional church workers takes money, and lots of it! So answering the question of *when* it is time to add staff is determined not only by the need of the congregation but also by its resources.

Most midsize churches are financially challenged, and so finding the funding for additional staff isn't easy. It also can be a risky venture, which is often the reason parishioners with high risk aversion and a cautious financial temperament are resistive to adding program staff. Yet such fiscal conservatism is not always the best practice of stewardship in a congregation. This is especially so when it means that refusing to add staff results in the failure to capitalize on wonderful opportunities to accomplish ministry and to advance God's mission.

When the congregation contemplates expanding its program staff, one important strategy is to view the adding of staff not as an additional financial burden but as an investment in growth. When these new staff positions are filled with qualified and competent candidates who are effectively deployed and appropriately supervised, in due time they will pay for themselves. It is generally agreed that the addition of a part-time staff person should generate increased revenue to cover her salary within one year, whereas a full-time

13.   McIntosh, *One Size Doesn't Fit All*, 151.
14.   Miller, *Navigating toward Maximum Effectiveness in Midsize Churches*, 18. Miller, *Coaching Midsize Congregations toward Positive Change*, 13.

person should do so within two to three years.[15] This increased revenue results from the increasing number of people participating in the programs that are catalyzed by the new staff person. These newcomers thereupon become financial contributors to the church. Up to that time, however, the congregation must subsidize the salary of the recently added staff person.

This return on the congregation's investment is not automatic, however, and depends on what kind of worker fills the staff position and how many people are reached by it. The key is to focus initially on staff positions that will clearly expand the reach of the congregation into new frontiers of ministry. Common positions in which a new staff worker will achieve this advancement of mission are these: coordinator of outreach and assimilation, service gifts manager, youth and children minister, family ministry facilitator, small group coordinator, missional community catalyst, and music ministry director.

This means that the congregation focuses on expansion, not on duplication. The new program staff should not simply assist the pastor in existing duties, merely providing relief to an overburdened cleric. Instead they should multiply ministry by reaching new people and equipping existing members to do outreach. They should be strategically focused to engage the unchurched in the surrounding community. They should also seek to increase the involvement of existing members, especially those who are relatively inactive in the life of the congregation.

Sometimes limited financial resources will force a congregation to look for creative and unconventional approaches to add staff workers. At least three options are possible here. The first is to acquire staff members who are willing to work without pay or at radically below-market wages. Obviously this implies that they have financial means other than what is provided by the church. Candidates in this regard include retired members of the congregation or retirees who are available in the community. Other candidates are people whose family income is sufficient because of a spouse's employment or because the worker has compensation through another job. Oftentimes these positions are part-time, and usually are filled by existing members of the congregation who see this program effort as their special mission. The congregation must be cautious not to take advantage of or exploit these workers.

The second funding option is to pay for the new staff member through agencies external to the church. This funding can be acquired through grants by faith-based foundations that require the congregation first to apply for the grant or to make a special request. It can also be received from benefactors who are approached by the congregation's representative, oftentimes the pastor. In both of these cases the church must take the initiative to "make the ask" for the funds. A helpful resource for this approach is William P. Dillon's book, *People Raising: A Practical Guide to*

15. Ibid. Martin, *The Myth of the 200 Barrier*, 107.

Raising Funds.[16] It should be noted, however, that most funding provided by an external agency will serve only as seed money for the initiative, not for ongoing sustainability. This is appropriate, since a healthy initiative should become self-sustaining within three years.

A third option is to utilize fixed-term appointments. Typically this involves the use of a ministry intern who serves for a limited period of time, such as for a year. Most schools of higher education which form students for ministerial vocations, such as seminaries and denominational colleges, require field education and internships for their students. Congregations can benefit from using these workers for a fixed period of time. Of course, a downside to this is that the position is temporary in duration.

When is it time to add program staff? The answer to that question depends on a number of variables regarding the congregation's size, needs, resources, and tolerance for risk. Whatever the case may be, the midsize church will require program and ministry staff beyond the lead shepherd. So sooner or later this question will be addressed. Usually it is healthier for the church to answer in the affirmative sooner rather than later. In the matter of adding staff, the (extra-biblical) proverb is usually true: He who hesitates is lost.

WHERE? NARROWING THE SOURCE FOR CANDIDATES

A critical question to be answered in the process of searching for church staff workers involves the question of *where*. Where will we look to find qualified candidates? The pool of potential candidates will need to be identified and then narrowed. Where will those candidates be found to begin the process of discerning which one or ones are best qualified for the position?

The first issue to be considered in this regard is whether the search process will focus on those within the congregation or those outside of it. Historically the predominant practice has been to look beyond the membership of the congregation for calling or hiring full-time church workers. This is because these workers have traditionally been viewed as professionals, and so the assumption is that they are to receive professional schooling. Such staff workers are secured either by interviewing candidates who are about to graduate from an educational institution (e.g., seminary, Bible school, religious university) or by searching for experienced professionals in the field. This search process provides some assurance that the candidate has appropriate theological competence and has been exposed to sociological theory and methodological resources to carry out her ministerial assignments competently. There is much to be commended to this traditional approach, and the fact that it remains a common practice attests to its ongoing value.

16.   William P. Dillon, *People Raising: A Practical Guide to Raising Funds* (Chicago: Moody, 2012).

However, a growing trend is for churches to look within their own memberships for paid staff workers. That is, they intentionally raise up workers from within. This homegrown approach is especially used in the case of securing part-time staff. But it can also be done to procure full-time program staff. Since many Christian universities and theological seminaries now have online educational offerings leading to either a certificate or a degree in ministry, frequently workers for churches are being formed *in situ* in their congregations while taking coursework at a distance from the educational institution. This approach has the advantage of forming professional church workers in a practice-reflection process.

Most commonly, however, the homegrown approach is used to secure part-time staff. These semi-professional positions are thereby filled with candidates who are raised up within the congregation. The advantage of this approach is that such indigenous staff workers are readily available and have a proven track record. Because they already are established in the congregation and community, there is less of an economic issue in terms of employing them part-time. In other words, the ministry tasks are attended to by locally available laypersons who demonstrate a passion for and ability to address a single task. The advantage here is that the indigenous worker is immediately familiar with the culture and inner workings of the church, so there is less of a learning curve and less risk of the appointment becoming a bad fit. Usually when one hires homegrown staff it is because they have proven themselves to be faithful and effective already; their temperament and work ethic has been approved by the faith community.[17]

Furthermore, it is not uncommon for such a position to morph over time. First the worker serves as a volunteer who proves her mettle and leads a programmatic initiative to grow. This growth in turn develops into a need for more substantive leadership of the program, which evolves into a reconfiguration of its leadership as a part-time paid position. If the effort continues to grow and demands more staff oversight, the hourly labor expectation (and commensurate financial compensation) also grows. Ultimately this has the potential to expand into a full-time position. In such a case the development of both the program and its leadership follows an organic trajectory.

There are, however, some potential disadvantages to the practice of employing existing members. Sometimes an indigenous worker will be so ingrained in the congregational culture that she is unable to think outside the box and may demonstrate tunnel vision. That worker may have limited experience in and exposure to creative ways of doing ministry. Gary McIntosh maintains: "A basic principle for adding staff says: If change is wanted, hire from without; if change is not wanted, hire from within."[18]

---

17.   The part-time configuration does not preclude formal training. Online and short-term intensive educational opportunities may bring great benefit to part-time workers, equipping them for greater theological, theoretical, and practical expertise.

18.   McIntosh, *Staff Your Church for Growth*, 46.

Another risk with employing existing members is the awkwardness of supervising staff workers who have pre-existing relationships and status in the congregation. Alice Mann identifies some of the problematic dynamics associated with employing staff from within:

> Hiring members is a tricky venture. It is harder to maintain clear lines of accountability when a staff member occupies other social roles in the system such as church member, longtime friend, or relative. Boundaries get fuzzy; for example, with whom should I discuss the ups and downs of the last staff meeting, or where am I free to complain if I hated that new hymn? Hiring of members only works in a healthy way when the employed person willingly relinquishes most of the prerogatives of "member" (e.g., "I may express an opinion on any issue") in favor of behaviors appropriate to the "staff member" role ("I voice concerns in staff meetings, then support the staff decision").[19]

It can be a challenge for a lead pastor or ministry supervisor to address problems with homegrown staff members. Due to the network of existing relationships in the congregation, it is difficult to dismiss those indigenous staff members who fail to accomplish their assigned responsibilities. "Once having experienced the pain of discharging a beloved long-term family member from a staff position," Gary McIntosh observes, "some churches prefer to add new staff from outside the congregation."[20] Accordingly, appropriately designed boundaries and expectations must be addressed proactively before existing members are brought on to the church's staff.

Where should a church look to find candidates for its staff positions? The answer to that question varies depending on the needs and context of the church, as well as its internal human resources. In some cases the congregation will look outside of its membership to fill the staff positions. In other cases future staff can be raised up within the church. Either option may be a viable one, depending on the circumstances. Nevertheless, the search committee will want to weigh the advantages and disadvantages of each option before choosing which path to follow.

WHO? IDENTIFYING THE PERSON

The fifth question to be addressed in the process of searching for new program staff in the midsize church is *who*—who will be chosen to fill this ministry position? This means to find the right person for the position. This involves the practice of discernment. As Christians seek to discern who is right for the ministry role, they will turn to the Lord in prayer. Certainly the search committee in its meetings will pray, but so also will the existing ministry staff, the other lay leaders, and the plenary

---

19.   Mann, *Raising the Roof*, 22.
20.   McIntosh, *Staff Your Church for Growth*, 47.

congregation when it gathers for worship. They will ask the Holy Spirit to guide the process and to lead them to a God-pleasing selection.

Five characteristics should be sought out in a candidate, no matter what the specific ministry position may be. Each characteristic begins with the letter *c*, forming an alliterated list. The qualities to be considered are consecration, character, competence, calling, and compatibility. In one of the first episodes involving the addition of ministry staff to the nascent church in Jerusalem, these characteristics were applied in selecting seven men to oversee the daily distribution of food to needy widows. Acts 6:2–4 describes the event in the following manner: "And the twelve summoned the full number of the disciples and said, 'It is not right that we should give up preaching the word of God to serve tables. Therefore, brothers, pick out from among you [compatibility] seven men of good repute [character], full of the Spirit [consecration] and of wisdom [competence], whom we will appoint to this duty [calling]. But we will devote ourselves to prayer and to the ministry of the word.'" The five characteristics of candidates are identified here as the qualifications for the selection of these workers who assist the apostles. We will examine each of these qualities in turn.

Consecration. This attribute concerns the candidate's spiritual disposition. The word derives from a Latin term meaning to be joined to the sacred. So it has to do with a person's relationship with God, her devotion to the Lord in faith and life. In the account from Acts 6 this qualification is identified as being reflected in one who is "full of the Spirit." A fervent faith in the Lord Jesus and the demonstration of spiritual maturity are the *sine qua non* for those who will lead in ministry.[21] Faith in Christ and faithfulness to his word must be demonstrated in the lives of those who oversee and lead ministry programs as church staff. One who is renewed by the gospel and who seeks to live according to God's will is the target for this search.

Character. Especially in the work of ministry, character counts! The apostles directed the Christian community in Jerusalem to "pick out from among you seven men of good repute" (Acts 6:3).[22] Character involves the demonstration of integrity, honesty, moral strength, self-discipline, and a good reputation. It means that a person lives virtuously and manifests in her life the fruit of the Holy Spirit (Gal. 5:22–23). This is related to the previous qualification in that good character is a product of the sanctified life of one rightly related to God.

---

21.   The Apostle Paul states that an overseer "must not be a recent convert" (1 Tim. 3:6) and "must hold firm to the trustworthy word as taught" (Titus 1:9). In a similar way deacons "must hold the mystery of the faith with a clear conscience" (1 Tim. 3:6, 9).

22.   It is significant that in the list of qualifications for church leaders in 1 Timothy 3:1–13, twenty-one out of twenty-six qualities bear directly upon this matter of character, such as these: "sober-minded, self-controlled, respectable, hospitable. . . not a drunkard, not violent but gentle, not quarrelsome, not a lover of money" (vv. 2–3). In a similar listing in Titus chapter one, fifteen of the sixteen qualifications relate to the leader's character. Essentially the leader is to be "above reproach" (1 Tim. 3:2; Titus 1:6, 7).

In order for people to follow a leader, they must trust her. One's trust-worthiness is cultivated by a record of integrity and selflessness. In the practice of Christian ministry, who you *are* is as important as what you *do*. My experience has convinced me that it is even more critical to select people of character than people who are experts in a task, since it is much easier to improve someone's abilities than to change their character.

Competence. The previous statement does not mean that ability is unimportant. It also is essential! The new staff worker should be able to accomplish the responsibilities assigned to her, as articulated in the ministry position description. This corresponds to the attribute of being "full of wisdom" in Acts 6:3. The Greek word translated as *wisdom* (*sophia*) signifies seasoned understanding that is put into effective practice.

Program staff candidates must demonstrate the aptitude to carry out the responsibilities of their assignment. They should manifest the requisite skills, or at least show the potential to develop them. Assessing such aptitude involves not only interviewing the candidate but receiving the reports of those who have worked with her. When it comes to discerning the competence of a candidate, I recommend that the search committee give more weight to what others say about the candidate's performance than to what the candidate says about herself.

Calling. The future staff person should demonstrate a sense of vocation to ministry, and especially to the specific tasks associated with the program position to be filled. A youth pastor loves working with teenagers and pines to see them follow Christ amidst the temptations of the adolescent years. A coordinator of outreach has a heart for the lost and inspires other church members to engage their friends and neighbors with the gospel. A music director not only performs on an instrument (such as the organ) but thrives in creating opportunities for others to exercise their musical talents to the glory of God. These are staff workers who show evidence that they view their roles as a calling, not just a career!

Accordingly, the search committee will look for the candidate to display a burning passion for a specific area of ministry.[23] No matter what the job description says, people will eventually configure their job responsibilities around their passions. Accordingly the task for the search committee is to find someone who is passionate about the specific target ministry. Such a person will be highly self-motivated to advance the agenda assigned to her.

Compatibility. A church ministry staff is by very definition collaborative. That is, people work together (co-labor) in shared ministry. Ideally,

---

23. In the account of the calling of the seven in Acts 6, all of those selected bear Greek names (Acts 6:5). It is likely that they had already demonstrated a passion to care for their fellow Hellenists who were neglected in the early church's food distribution.

they will work together as a unified team. This means that it is beneficial if the staff members are compatible with each other from the start.[24]

In what areas are church workers to demonstrate compatibility? First, there is to be *theological* agreement. Since theology informs and actually forms practice, it is important that all the members of a church professional team be in accord regarding the basic theological matrix in which the practice of ministry is carried out. Second, there is to be *missional* alignment. Staff members need to be on board regarding the mission of the church so that everyone's programs are moving in the same missional direction. Third, there needs to be *personal* compatibility. This is a less tangible dynamic, but it is real and needed. Essentially it means that co-workers are team players, working in a cooperative manner. It means they are not independent, strong headed, and pushing of personal agendas. It also means that there is a good chemistry among the teammates. The personality and temperament of a new staff person should mesh well with that of others on the staff. These are all areas of compatibility that a search committee will consider when adding professional or paraprofessional workers to the multi-member staff of a midsize church.

Who is to fill the staff position? Many variables will inform that decision. But broadly speaking, those entrusted with the task of searching for candidates will look for these characteristics: consecration, character, competence, calling, and compatibility. By considering each of these attributes, the search team will be able to narrow the field so that a call can be extended or an offer made to a highly qualified candidate.

SUMMARY

A fundamental characteristic distinguishing a medium-sized congregation from a small one is that it requires a ministry staff of multiple members, whereas the "pastoral size" church can be managed by only one person—the pastor. When the average attendance of worshippers exceeds 150, a tipping point occurs in which one person is no longer able to handle all of the needs and expectations of the parishioners, and so additional program staff must be added.

The addition of staff relieves the lead pastor of some duties, but also brings new responsibilities and challenges. An important dimension to the process of adding program staff is to do so with thoughtfulness and intentionality. This process will be guided by attention to five matters. First, the congregation must carefully identify the purpose of the position—*why* it

---

24. Compatibility does not mean being the same. In a healthy marriage the wife and husband are compatible, but they are hardly the same. They bring their distinctive differences, some of which are gender based, to the marriage union. So also among the members of a church staff there are many differences in giftedness, perspective, and methodology. These enrich the team and help it to become more than the sum of its parts.

is needed. Second, the staff role must be defined using a ministry position description so that all parties are clear about *what* is expected of this new worker. Third, congregational leaders will discern *when* it is appropriate to add more staff, depending on the church's need and the resources. Fourth, the search team will narrow the source field for the candidates, agreeing on *where* they will look to find the best potential worker. Fifth, the process will lead to the identification of *who* is most qualified to fill the position to advance the ministry and mission of the congregation.

The acquisition of employed personnel is critical to the effective functioning of a medium-sized church. Yet the professional staff exists not to monopolize the work of the church, but to multiply it. Each staff worker is called upon "to equip the saints for the work of ministry" (Eph. 4:12). This means to garner the participation of laypeople for ministry as well. Such an opportunity is the focus of the next chapter.

CHAPTER 9

PARTICIPATION

After some months of engaging in a search process, the members of Faith Church called Shauna Martin to serve as its Director of Education and Youth. Pastor Andrew Burke saw this new chapter in the life of the congregation as an occasion to seek guidance from a consultant on how to work well together as a church staff team. Dr. Jasmine Kouri, a professor at a nearby Christian college, was selected to guide the newly formed staff in team formation. Dr. Kouri met weekly with the four church staff members, two of which were full-time—Pastor Burke and Shauna—and two of which were part-time—Jacob, the Director of Music Ministry, and Gillian, the Service Gifts Coordinator.

Several months into this process, during a regularly scheduled consultation session with the staff of Faith Church, Dr. Kouri commented, "I rejoice with you that you have entered into this partnership as staff. I think the Apostle Paul's reference to a partnership in the gospel in Philippians is being evidenced in your shared labor. But I want you to notice something about this scriptural passage to which I just now referred. It is found in Philippians chapter one. Would one of you read verses three through five out loud for us all?"

Jacob volunteered. He read, "I thank my God in all my remembrance of you, always in every prayer of mine for you all making my prayer with joy, because of your partnership in the gospel from the first day until now."

"Thank you, Jake," Jasmine Kouri continued. "In this passage when Paul speaks of your partnership in the gospel, the pronoun *your* is plural in form. He is addressing a group of people. He also states that he thanks God for *you all*, also indicating a plurality. So who is the *you all* that Paul is referring to here?"

Gillian, the Service Gifts Coordinator, responded. "I guess it is all the people of the church in Philippi to whom the apostle is writing."

"Right you are!" replied Professor Kouri. "Notice the greeting at the beginning of the letter. Verse one states, 'Paul and Timothy, servants of Christ Jesus, to *all the saints* in Christ Jesus who are at Philippi, with the overseers and deacons.'

Now the overseers and deacons identified are workers like you; they are the staff of the church. In the first century they didn't use terms like professional staff, yet we can draw a general equivalence. But the ones to whom Paul writes are more than the overseers and deacons. He is writing to *all* the saints at Philippi! That includes what we today would call the lay people. And so the laity is very much included in what the apostle refers to as the *partnership in the gospel*."

Pastor Burke interjected his approval of this interpretation. "Your exegesis of these verses is sound, good professor! But what is your point for us today?"

Jasmine answered, "My point is that what Paul here calls a partnership, or what we in these past several months of discussion have called the team, extends beyond your staff. The team that is assigned the work of the gospel is the entire church—the whole congregation! It includes your lay people. The men, women, and children who fill Faith Church's membership rolls are to be part of this partnership in the gospel ministry. And it is your responsibility to engage them in that partnership. It is your calling to equip them for the work of ministry, as the Apostle Paul states elsewhere in Ephesians chapter four."

Dr. Kouri continued. "You can't function alone, nor should you. Your role as a staff is to equip others for ministry in the name of Christ. You are to engage the lay members of Faith Church to share in the partnership of the gospel ministry. But the task is not easy. Your assignment to enlist others to participate in mission and ministry is a challenging one. Yet it can be done, and it must be done. Remember that verse in Philippians about the partnership in the gospel? Well, the very next verse identifies where the power comes from for carrying out that partnership. Shauna, please read aloud verse six of Philippians chapter one."

Shauna Martin picked up her tablet and read from her Bible app: "'And I am sure of this, that he who began a good work in you will bring it to completion at the day of Jesus Christ.' Yes, I see! God is the one who is doing the work of the gospel. We are partnering with him!"

"Indeed!" Professor Kouri affirmed. "Paul states that God is doing this work in us, and that means that he is also doing his work through us in this world. That's his promise. It's by his power! But he is doing it not just through the 'overseers and deacons,' not just through the professional church staff. He does it through all his saints. And he has given you the privilege and power now to mobilize them to do it! The saints at Faith Church are to participate in this partnership in the gospel."

Gillian nodded her head in agreement. "What you have shared with us here, Professor Kouri, is very dear to my heart. In my role as Coordinator of Service Gifts, helping lay people use their gifts in the service of the gospel is what I am charged to do. I know that this is what God wants done; as you have pointed out, the Bible is clear about that. But how do we take the leap from theology to practice? How do we in practical terms mobilize our lay people?"

Dr. Kouri smiled. "That, my friends, will be our next quest of discovery."

EXPANDING PARTICIPATION TO THE LAITY

Any size of church—small, medium, and large—can and should involve the lay membership in its mission and ministry. The Bible not only assumes this, it affirms it (e.g., Acts 2:42–45; Rom. 12:1–8; 1 Cor. 12:1–30; Gal. 6:9–10; Eph. 4:11–16; 1 Peter 2:4–10).

There no doubt are some clergy and professional church leaders who dismiss this biblical mandate to mobilize the baptized for mission and ministry. Perhaps they wish to monopolize the work of the church. Some may be threatened by the idea of sharing leadership with others. Others may simply not trust lay people to carry out the work of ministry faithfully or effectively. Whatever the reason, these professional leaders restrict the work of ministry and thus severely limit the church's potential for influence and impact in its mission.

But my observation is that this phenomenon is not common. Most professional church leaders—pastors and program staff—desire greatly to involve the laity in the work of the church. The challenge, however, is *how* to do so. There are many obstacles to engaging the laity, even if clergy desire to do so. Indeed, one of the most common laments from pastors and other program staff in churches is how few lay workers participate in the work of the congregation.

PARTICIPATION BEYOND THE PREMISES

The participation of the laity in the mission and ministry of the local congregation is a desirable objective. Indeed, the plan of God is that pastors and staff "equip the saints for the work of ministry, for building up the body of Christ, until we all attain to the unity of the faith and of the knowledge of the Son of God, to mature manhood, to the measure of the stature of the fullness of Christ" (Eph. 4:11–13). God intends that all his baptized people engage in being nurtured in faith and serve others as the fruit of faith. This builds up the body of Christ and unifies believers in faith and spiritual maturity.

This does not mean, however, that a layperson's *diakonia*—the word translated as *ministry* in Ephesians 4:12—is always and only done within the official programmatic efforts of the local congregation. This is a fallacy that should be dispelled. Participation in the work of the Lord is not restricted to those activities sponsored by the church. Participation in ministry goes beyond the premises of the parish! In fact, Christians are very much about their Father's business when they carry out what God calls them to do in their everyday lives at home, in the workplace, and in their communities. This is the biblical teaching on vocation that was rediscovered in the Reformation.[1]

The Reformers recognized that God does not remove his baptized saints from the world, but sends them into the world as his agents of providence and mercy. The most immediate opportunities for this ministry are in the various everyday contexts of life. Each Christian has a number of vocations: serving as a son, daughter, sibling, parent, neighbor, citizen, employee, employer, etc. These are the contexts of first importance for living out mission and ministry. They are true callings, for God has given people these roles to serve one another in God's stead and by his authorization.

Martin Luther referred those who live out their vocations as masks of God. This means that God is behind the faithful work of a mother preparing supper, or a son mowing the lawn, or a farmer harvesting crops, or a sanitary collector gathering garbage, or a surgeon replacing a hip, or a waiter serving a meal. God upholds and sustains his creation through human creatures acting as his agents of blessing. Christians see these roles and responsibilities for what they are—holy vocations. As they carry out these callings faithfully, they are doing the work of God.

A corollary teaching to the doctrine of vocation, also emphasized in the Reformation, is that of the priesthood of all believers.[2] This doctrine affirms that all Christians, by virtue of their baptisms, are priests of God. Just as clergy are installed into their office by the rite of ordination, so also every Christian is installed into a priestly office by baptism. The Apostle Peter affirms this identity when he writes to lay Christians: "But you are a chosen race, a royal *priesthood*, a holy nation, a people for his [God's] own possession, that you may proclaim the excellencies of him who called you out of darkness into his marvelous light" (1 Peter 2:9, emphasis mine).

Oftentimes people associate the priesthood of the baptized only with the ability to approach and address God directly through the merits of Christ. This is certainly a glorious application of this doctrine, but it does not exhaust its content. What is emphasized in the passage from 1 Peter just quoted is the role that every Christian priest has to declare forth the wondrous saving work of God. The word translated *proclaim* here means literally to announce out (*exangeilēte*) what God has done to rescue humans. It is not speaking only about praising God for his redemptive work in the vertical relationship, but it is speaking especially about declaring out to others this message in their horizontal relationships. Peter

---

1. Helpful expositions of this doctrine are provided in Gene Veith, *God at Work: Your Christian Vocation in All of Life* (Wheaton: Crossway, 2011); D. M. Bennethum, *Listen! God is Calling!: Luther Speaks of Vocation, Faith, and Work* (Minneapolis: Augsburg Fortress, 2003); and Timothy Keller, *Every Good Endeavor: Connecting Your Work to God's Work* (New York: Penguin, 2014).

2. See Jacob Preus, III, "The Holy Ministry and the Holy Priesthood: The Gospel Office and the Office from the Gospel," *Concordia* 24 (1998): 36–42.

is saying that the Christian identity as God's priest is for the purpose of bearing witness to our deliverance from the darkness of sin that God has effected through the work of Christ.

Just as in the Old Testament a primary role of the priests and Levites was to proclaim and teach about God and his will (Lev. 10:11; Deut. 33:10), so every Christian has this priestly privilege to carry out in his everyday vocations. And just as a priest of the Old Covenant was the representative of God to other humans, so now every baptized believer serves as God's intermediary to the world by bearing witness to the work and word of the Lord.

Peter in his epistle goes on to make clear that the practice of this priesthood is conducted primarily not within the walls of the gathered assembly of saints, but in the contexts of their everyday witness to the world. He exhorts his readers: "Keep your conduct among the Gentiles honorable, so that. . . they may see your good deeds and glorify God on the day of visitation" (1 Peter 2:12). Peter proceeds to identify some of the specific contexts in which Christians exercise their priestly roles of witness: in the civil realm as citizens (1 Peter 2:13–17), in the workplace as employees (1 Peter 2:18–25), in the home as wives and husbands (1 Peter 3:1–7). In other words, the priestly function of witness in word and deed is carried out in our everyday vocations.

Certainly Christian laypeople's participation in the mission of God and the ministry of the church is not limited to activities that happen within the walls of the church facility. Participation indeed is beyond the premises! Pastors do a disservice to the laity when they associate the work of the church only with volunteerism in the official programmatic efforts of the congregation. This can foster a disconnection between faith and life. It can reduce ministry only to efforts that lay people exert on the premises of the parish.

PARTICIPATION ON THE PREMISES

But the call to lay participation doesn't *exclude* the possibility that ministry by the laity may be done on the church premises! Much of the Lord's work can be done, indeed must be done, when saints are gathered together under the auspices of the local congregation.

Peter makes this clear as well, writing the following in chapter four of his first epistle: "Above all, keep loving one another earnestly, since love covers a multitude of sins. Show hospitality to one another without grumbling. As each has received a gift, use it to serve one another, as good stewards of God's varied grace: whoever speaks, as one who speaks oracles of God; whoever serves, as one who serves by the strength that God supplies—in order that in everything God may be glorified through Jesus Christ. To him belong glory and dominion forever and ever. Amen" (1 Peter 4:8–11). The coupling of words that reoccur in this passage is *one another*. Since Peter is writing to Christians, clearly the reference applies to those who gather regularly to speak and hear God's word. It refers to believers who assemble to serve and care for one another. That context of the gathering place is on the premises of the local congregation.

There is a time and place for Christians to gather together around God's word and the sacraments to be nurtured by these means of grace. God desires that believers meet together to encourage each other and "to stir up one another to love and good works" (Heb. 10:24–25). Like the early church in Jerusalem, Christians today gather in congregations for worship, instruction, fellowship, prayer, the sharing of needs and goods, service, and outreach (Acts 2:42–47). This is especially where the programmatic ministry of the local parish comes into play. This is where the participation of lay people on the premises is a God-pleasing thing. It is where Christian sisters and brothers may encourage, uphold, edify, and enlighten *one another*. It is where they can join forces corporately to advance God's mission in the world.

THE PARTICULAR NEED FOR LAY PARTICIPATION IN THE MIDDLE-SIZED PARISH

In the midsize church, the need for increased lay participation is especially acute. Similarly, the struggle to involve volunteers can be particularly challenging. This is more critical in a medium church than in a small or large one.

The functions of the small church revolve around the activity of the pastor. That is why it has been labeled *pastoral* size. In a small church the pastor executes much of the efforts of the congregation. Accordingly, when lay people are little involved in leadership roles, the congregation still can function adequately simply by depending on the pastor.

The large church is different in that leadership and management do not revolve around only one person. In the corporate-size church the congregational initiatives are led and managed by a professional staff that is overseen by the lead pastor. Yet there is a similarity with the small church. Alice Mann has demonstrated that both pastoral-size (small) and corporate-size (large) churches are pastor-centered.[3] Ministry and mission are highly professionalized and staff-driven. Thus a large church can function adequately, although certainly not optimally, with the paid staff doing the bulk of the work of ministry.

This dynamic contrasts dramatically with what occurs in the middle-sized church. The congregational system centers its life on the group rather than on a pastor and the professional staff. Alice Mann describes this dynamic as follows:

> A new kind of teamwork becomes necessary in an uneven leadership matrix in which some programs have paid staff, some have volunteer leaders so dedicated that they function like staff, and some have committees at the helm. Board and

---

3.   Mann, *The In-Between Church*, 20–23.

pastor must find ways to keep the parts connected with each other *directly*—in horizontal networks of collaboration—not just *indirectly* through board reports and liaisons. As in a spider web, the center of this leadership network does not consist of a single point (the pastor) but of a small circle (half a dozen key program leaders—paid and unpaid, clergy and lay) led by the pastor.[4]

Simply put, the administration of the congregation must be more broadly shared in the medium church as compared to small or large parishes. The participation of lay people is essential!

The midsize church is characterized by a proliferation of programs. These multiple programs must be led and managed by *someone*. Most medium congregations don't have the resources to pay personnel to direct all of these programs. Accordingly, many of the programs will need to be attended to by volunteer lay members. There is an especially acute need to expand the base of lay participation in the program-size church.

ENLISTING LAY LEADERS

One of the greatest needs in contemporary North American society is to engender leaders. Observers of many different social sectors—government, business, commerce, military, non-profit, domestic—have heralded this need. This challenge certainly exists in the ecclesial realm as well. And the need is not only for more and better professional leadership by clergy and church staff workers. The need is great for lay leaders in Christian congregations. The enlistment of lay leaders is essential to a positive future for the medium-sized church.

This chapter focuses on how to raise up lay leaders to meet these needs. This is a significant challenge in North American context. Most lay members of congregations are extremely busy in their personal and professional lives. They are also oftentimes highly committed—even over-committed—to activities such as athletics, hobbies, leisure, and personal interests that compete with opportunities to participate in the body life of the church. People's time and availability can be stringently restricted.

Yet there is the promise of abundant blessing and extraordinary fulfillment to those people who offer their God-given gifts and service to the purposes of their church. So how can the laity become more engaged in these opportunities for service and witness in the name of their local congregation?

IDENTIFYING POTENTIAL LEADERS

The first step in broadening the participation of the laity in leadership is to identify congregational members who demonstrate the potential to lead.

---

4. Ibid., 22.

First the church must identify *who* might lead so that they can then be equipped to lead.

Recipients of Ministry

The pool of potential candidates for lay leaders will obviously include members who have been involved in the church for some time. These people have proven themselves to have some commitment to the body life of the church by attending worship services regularly. They also may attend other activities or programmatic offerings of the congregation. They might have attended congregation-wide social events. They may be recipients of that which is provided by the programmatic ministries offered by the church, such as the family ministry or the care ministry. They may have participated in fellowship groups such as a women's auxiliary.

In cases like these the lay member is functioning as a consumer. He is predominantly receiving from what the congregation has to offer. It is usually best to move such a person to a higher level of involvement and commitment before recruiting him to be a leader in the church.

Participants in Supportive Roles

The next kind of lay participant will have made some significant contribution of time and service to the ministry of the church. He is not only a receiver, but he gives of himself. He may have participated in a missional initiative such as a local outreach effort or a short-term mission trip. He may have volunteered for some kind of service to the community that is done in the name of the church. He may have played a supportive role in some aspect of the congregation's life together, such as serving on the praise team, acting as an usher, tending to tables in a fellowship event, or participating as a youth counselor. This lay member may have already participated on a committee or action team as a contributor but not a leader. Such a willingness to give of his time and abilities signals the appropriate attitude from which leaders can be developed.

Some congregations use processes and instruments to help members discover and execute the distinctive gifts for service that God has entrusted to them. Gillian, the part-time staff worker depicted earlier in this chapter, has been entrusted by Faith Church with the role of Service Gifts Coordinator. In this capacity she assists the members of her congregation in identifying their giftedness and in finding places to exercise their gifts. On occasion the discernment process will identify those who have the gifts of leadership and administration, and these should be designated as candidates for leadership positions. Kevin Martin, citing the theory of Edwin Friedman, maintains that in most congregations about ten percent of the worshipping community is truly gifted for leadership.[5] Whatever

---

5.   Martin, *The Myth of the 200 Barrier*, 99.

the actual proportion is, the congregation will seek to identify and enlist those who have the innate propensity to lead.

Influencers

One does not need to have a formal process of gift discovery in a congregation to identify those who demonstrate an aptitude to lead. What is necessary is the ability to recognize those who are influential in the church. The exercise of leadership is essentially the execution of influence—influencing people to work together toward a common purpose or goal. So one way to find people to fill formal leadership roles is to identify those who are already leading informally. Indeed, sometimes in the midsize church the most influential leaders are not in the boardrooms where formal decisions are made. They are the ones who are influencing opinions during the fellowship hour on Sunday morning or among the choir members during the rehearsals.

The key is to identify these influencers and then align their influence with the strategic direction of the parish. When informal influencers are mobilized for formal projects or initiatives in the church, their leadership skills will usually require little development, but they will need direction.

New Members

The previous paragraphs have located a pool of potential candidates for lay leaders from the members who have been involved in the church for some time. But there is another source that should not be overlooked. That is from among new members.

A phenomenon that frequently accompanies stagnation in a congregation's missional vitality is that long-tenured leaders are recycled through the available leadership positions. This means that the plenary pool of formal leaders—board directors and committee chairpersons—remains static. Sure, the occupants of these leadership positions change, but it is basically a reshuffling of the deck. The same individuals from the same dominant families recirculate the official leadership roster. My observation is that typically their motive for doing so is not to monopolize control of power in the congregation, although this can happen. No, these workers are consecrated Christians who truly want the church to flourish. So these faithful veterans re-up for leadership roles over and over again. What results, however, is a leadership system in the parish that remains constant and static, and so the dynamics of creativity and responsiveness to the community are oftentimes lost.

For this reason it is wise to seek out leaders proactively from among newcomers to the church. This is where the pastor and other staff workers play a pivotal role. Herb Miller observes that in small churches clergy primarily *accept* the lay leadership that is already a given in the congregation; that is, pastors learn to work with the leaders who are already established in roles of influence. However, in medium churches the clergy have much more opportunity to *select* lay leaders.[6] The pastor of the medium-sized church will exercise courageous leadership by aggressively identifying and recruiting leaders from those who have been members for five years or less.

Non-Members

In some cases emerging leaders may not even be members of the parish in the sense of having their names affixed to the membership roster. Increasingly it is the case that people who become involved in the church see little value in official membership. They are not concerned about the formalities of joining an organization such as a church.[7]

For this reason, the congregation should establish as few barriers as possible for these folks to participate in parish life, recognizing that they are on the path to deepening connections. This includes appropriate roles of leadership. Certainly some boundaries will need to be set. The task of teaching the faith must be entrusted to those who confess sound doctrine (see 2 Tim. 2:1–2; James 3:1). Leadership roles requiring significant spiritual maturity, such as lay elders, should be assigned only to those who have a track record of faithfulness to God's word and will. The pastor and staff will discern the appropriate requirements for the various leadership roles of the congregation. But any limitations to the involvement of newcomers, even those who have not formally joined the church, should be maintained not merely for the sake of the traditions and conventions of the local congregation but for the sake of the Lord's mission.

RECRUITING LEADERS

Once a pool of potential leaders is identified, a process of recruitment commences.

They must be *asked* to lead. Emerging leaders need to be invited to lead, or they likely will not participate. This may seem like a simple step in the process. Many assume that a quick request to serve, transmitted via email or text message, will do the job of recruitment. But that quick and easy approach can actually thwart a positive outcome in the enlistment process. When done rightly, the task of asking is much more deliberate and personal.

The basic task involved with inviting a candidate to assume a leadership role in the congregation is one of *persuasion*. It is critical that the one who asks another to lead does so in a persuasive manner.

Some pious Christians may object to this approach. They see it as manipulative and worldly, hardly befitting of the followers of Christ. They may assume that to actively persuade someone to serve in the church is to

---

6. Miller, *Coaching Midsize Congregations toward Positive Change*, 42.

7. David Peter, "The Challenge of Church Membership in the Twenty-First Century: Old and New Directions," in *Inviting Community*, ed. Robert Kolb and Theodore Hopkins (St. Louis: Concordia Seminary Press, 2013), 159–77.

infringe on the work of the Holy Spirit. These concerns have some merit, since the sinful flesh can emerge in such behavior and the recruiter may move into salesmanship that does not befit the name of Jesus. But this does not mean that persuasion *per se* is problematic. It is not inherently evil. The Apostle Paul identified his *modus operandi* for mission as persuasion (2 Cor. 5:11; see also Acts 18:4; 19:8; 26:27–28). So also today sanctified persuasion can be applied in the process of recruiting leaders. Indeed, the optimal outcome usually requires it.

What is the candidate for leadership to be persuaded of? Essentially, the recruiter will need to persuade him of two things. First, he will be persuaded of the importance and potential impact of the role. In this sense he will be recruited ultimately not to a *position*, such as the title of being chairperson of the Board for Youth Ministry. Instead, he will be recruited to a *cause*, such as the effort to ensure the spiritual vitality and faith formation of teenagers in the congregation. The recruiter will emphasize the impact that this role of leadership might have in keeping young people close to Christ and connected to his church. Busy people today are most likely to devote themselves to efforts that they perceive will make a positive difference in the lives of others, for time and for eternity. This is the case that must be made while asking someone to lead. And it must be made persuasively.

The second case that must be persuasively made is that the candidate being recruited is the best person available to lead the cause. Emphasize to him that he is recognized by the church to have the prerequisite qualifications to lead—he is able, he is godly, and he is trusted. The recruiter should emphasize that the selection of the candidate did not result from an arbitrary and slipshod process, but it was done through careful observation of his behavior and through critical analysis of his potential to lead. Moreover, it should be shared that the process of discernment was accompanied by much prayer, and so those who request his leadership believe that it will be met with God's blessing. The candidate should be asked likewise to consider prayerfully this opportunity to lead as a calling from God.

Thirdly, the recruiter will seek to assure the potential leader of the support of the congregation in his efforts. Staff support, financial support, and programmatic support will be highlighted. The candidate should be confident that the congregation has his back.

No doubt at this point the recruit will have many questions. The need for these to be answered promptly should be respected by the recruiter. The recruiter will also offer some time for the candidate to reflect upon this proposition and to pray about it. During that period of time the recruiter should make himself available for further discussion. It is best, however, that a deadline for a decision be identified as early in the process as possible, ideally the deadline is set during the initial meeting.

The key here is that the one making the proposal does so in a persuasive manner. This will communicate the seriousness and thoughtfulness that went into the selection of the candidate for the position. This effort at persuasion, appropriately offered, will greatly increase the probability that the recruit will accept the leadership position. It will also contribute to a more favorable start to his leadership experience that will follow.

EQUIPPING LEADERS

When a recruit has agreed to serve in a leadership role in the church, this doesn't mean that he is immediately ready to lead. In fact, throwing a novice into a leadership role unprepared and leaving him to sink or swim can lead to disaster. It may result in an unnecessary failure that is detrimental to the congregation's ministry. Even worse, it may lead to a frustrating experience that discourages the recruit from further participation in the church's work.

The emerging leader in the midsize church needs to be equipped for the leadership role he assumes. He is to learn not only how to lead, but more specifically how to do so in the specific context of his service. Leadership always involves learning. Even the most seasoned leaders are constantly learning, especially if they begin a new context of leadership. Nascent leaders need to be equipped for the task. This involves the process of gaining information about, experience with, and expertise in the functions of leadership. That requires learning.

There are four dynamics at play in this equipping process. Although they follow to some degree a logical progression, they are not absolutely sequential. This is a recursive process, not an exclusively linear one, in which each dynamic is at play to a greater or lesser degree through much of the time of development. The four dynamics are instruction, immersion, imitation, and innovation.[8] We will now examine each of these dynamics and see how they may be enacted in a leadership formation process in the midsize church.

Instruction
The first step in the equipping process is to provide the necessary information about the area of responsibility assigned to the new leader. This is frequently delivered through instruction. That instruction can be face to face, in a group setting, online using pre-recorded video, or via other venues. Often it is supported with some reading resources. Some of the information may be theological in nature. Scriptural and doctrinal instruction is critical to forming spiritually mature leaders; it helps them to understand the *what* and *why* of ministry. Other material may be more practical. This provides them with insight into methods and best

---

8. The equivalent of three of these dynamics—information, imitation, innovation—is developed in Mike Breen, *Multiplying Missional Leaders: From Half-hearted Volunteers to a Mobilized Kingdom Force* (Pawleys Island, SC: 3dm, 2012), 83–85.

practices, the *how* of ministry. The desired outcome is that the new leader is familiarized with the nature of his responsibilities as well as policies and procedures of the organization.

Certainly a new leader should be instructed about the *ends* for the position that he assumes. He is informed about what outcomes are expected from the ministry team he will lead, that is, what they are accountable to accomplish. These objectives should be clearly identified, preferably in writing. They may be articulated in the church's bylaws or in in the parish's strategic plan. They may simply be written by a professional staff person for a given initiative. This helps the nascent leader to grasp what is expected of him and of the group he leads. It enables him to envision what his group effort is to produce.

The leader in training is also instructed about the *limitations* of authority and resources for this position. He is familiarized with the boundaries of the position's scope. He is informed regarding the resources—finances, facilities, communication media, staff support—available to him for this ministry effort. Ethical and legal policies should be communicated to him at this time.

Emerging leaders may also receive information on the subject of leadership itself. There are many resources available in this regard, both from the ecclesial and the secular realms.[9]

The need for instruction for how to lead is most critical at the beginning of the learning process. But it isn't limited to that stage. Good leaders are constantly learning through new information. They continually seek helpful instruction.

Immersion

The second dynamic in the process of equipping lay leaders is that of providing them with field experience. Most people learn leadership skills best in a context of practice-reflection, all of which takes place as they become immersed in the assigned effort. Leaders best learn the culture and values of the congregational program by being immersed in ministry. They acquire insight into important traditions and practices. As they actually set foot on the journey, the desired destination is transformed from

---

9. An example is John Maxwell's website, www.INJOY.com. Helpful books on Christian leadership include the following: Benjamin Forrest and Chet Roden, eds., *Biblical Leadership: Theology for the Everyday Leader* (Grand Rapids: Kregel, 2017); Rod Woods, *Freed to Lead: How Your Identity in Christ Can Transform Any Leadership Role* (Grand Rapids: Monarch Books, 2016); Richard Rardin, *The Servant's Guide to Leadership* (Brentwood, PA: Selah, 2001); Scott Cormode, *Making Spiritual Sense: Christian Leaders as Spiritual Interpreters* (Nashville: Abingdon, 2006); James M. Kouzes and Barry Z. Posner, *Christian Reflections on the Leadership Challenge* (San Francisco: Jossey-Bass, 2004); Lovett H. Weems, *Church Leadership*, rev. ed. (Nashville: Abingdon, 2010); Tim Elmore, *Habitudes: Images that Form Leadership Habits and Attitudes* (Atlanta: Growing Leaders, 2006–2009); James C. Galvin, *I've Got Your Back: A Leadership Parable* (Elgin, IL: Tenth Power, 2012).

theory to reality. It is through instruction that the nature of leadership is taught. It is through immersion that it is caught.

This immersive dynamic can be compared to the experience of learning to swim. One can read books and articles about swimming, but he doesn't really know how to swim until he gets into a pool and is immersed in water. There he learns the necessary strokes by actually moving his arms and legs, all under the supervision and guidance of an experienced swimmer. Similarly, emerging leaders will best learn how to navigate in leadership by being immersed in the activity—by doing it—but also with supervision, guidance, and modeling. It is my opinion that leadership is best apprehended not in the classroom, where information is received, but in the field, where experience is gained. This on-the-job-training is a fertile environment for growth in leadership capacity.

Emerging leaders today will benefit from immersion in ministry under the mentorship of another before taking the reins of sole leadership. Immersion in the context of the actual practice of leadership is an effective proving ground for leadership formation.

Imitation

For centuries people have recognized that a rich context for learning how to lead involves the process of apprenticeship. Certainly apprenticeships are useful in technical schools for trades such as carpentry, plumbing, and electrical work. But actually it is an approach that is highly beneficial to leadership formation in the professions, in government, and in the church. Oftentimes in these latter contexts the term used is *mentorship*, but the approach is essentially the same.

Engaging the dynamic of imitation means that the emerging leader is primed for greater responsibility by first practicing limited leadership in partnership with and under the guidance of another more experienced leader. The veteran leader will model effective leadership skills and practices that in turn the emerging leader integrates into his own style for leading. The learner observes how the veteran leader operates, and imitates that behavior. This is a powerful way to replicate leadership.

People typically learn skills best by imitation. This involves observation and collaboration. Let me provide an illustration. I enjoy doing handyman work in our house and yard. When an item needs repair or renovation, I will seek out information that will equip me with the skills to successfully address that need. I used to consult how-to books to read about the steps that need to be taken. But now I usually go online and watch a video of someone who shows me how to successfully complete the project. Best of all is to access a skilled friend who comes over and shows me how to get started and then guides me as I do some of the work. When the friend sees that I have gained the necessary DIY (do-it-yourself) skill, he takes his leave and I continue my project. I progress at accomplishing the task simply because I am imitating my friend's technique. Sometimes I have to call him with concerns or questions along the way. If I really come to a place where I'm stumped on how to progress further, he will make another visit. But most of the time the task is completed successfully. I have great satisfaction not only in having fixed the plumbing or in having installed the flooring, but also in having gained the skills for doing so—skills that I can continue to use in the future.

Not only can one learn the skills for home improvement through this method of imitation, one can learn skills for leadership improvement. The process of imitation essentially follows this progression:

1. The accomplished leader demonstrates the skill and the assumptive leader observes how it is done.
2. The seasoned leader and the learner carry out the task together, collaborating on the project in an interactive manner.
3. The emerging leader does the primary work of leadership while the veteran leader watches, intervening occasionally to provide some correction or direction.
4. The new leader carries out the task of leadership using his honed skills, reporting the results to his mentor.

Because of the importance that imitation plays in forming new lay leaders, I recommend that the organizational structure of the congregation intentionally promote this. Emerging leaders are formally paired with experienced leaders in an apprenticeship or mentorship relationship. This way the apprentices not only learn the nuts and bolts of ministry, but they also witness firsthand how leadership is incarnated in the persons of their mentors. Best of all, it is an environment that effectively forms leadership skills while also cultivating supportive relationships between the participants.[10]

Innovation

The fourth dynamic at play in the process of developing lay leaders is that of innovation. This means that the emerging leader not only replicates the style and skill of his mentor, but he creates his own distinctive approach to leadership. The goal of the process of leadership development is not to clone leaders; it is to create them. God's creation demonstrates a wondrous diversity. So also in this creative process there will result leaders with diverse approaches and contributions.

In his book, *Multiplying Missional Leaders*, Mike Breen describes the transition from imitation to innovation. He addresses the mentors of emerging leaders as follows: "For a while someone will imitate and copy what you do, but eventually they come to a base level of competency and can start *Innovation*. They innovate through the lens of their personality.

---

10. Phil Newton, *The Mentoring Church: How Pastors and Congregations Cultivate Leaders* (Grand Rapids: Kregel, 2017).

They innovate through the lens of their missional context. They innovate as the Holy Spirit shapes them and leads them. The ultimate point is not that a person looks exactly like you. The point is they start there so they can get to the flexibility of innovation."[11]

The benefits of innovation are manifold. First, innovation brings advancement. Imagine that a lay leader is mentored to become the new chairperson of the Board of Youth Ministry. By imitating his predecessor he will bring continuity to the effective functioning of that board. But by innovating in his leadership he will bring the board—and the youth ministry it directs—to a new level of effectiveness. His innovative leadership will enable the board not only to maintain its momentum but also to advance new initiatives. It empowers progress beyond what had been achieved earlier. Another way of saying this is that the innovation brings improvement. It brings even better solutions to existing problems, better resolution to existing needs, better delivery of ministry.

A second benefit of innovation is that it cultivates reflexivity to the context. In our fast-changing society, Christians must respond to the changing needs of people with adroitness. In its mission to engage the ever-changing culture with the never-changing gospel, the church is especially in need of innovative leaders. This is why it is often good to develop leaders who are newcomers to the congregation. They may have a more acute awareness of emerging needs than do existing leaders who can become restricted by paradigm paralysis.

A third benefit of innovation is that it generates reformation. This is demonstrated in the maxim *Ecclesia semper reformanda est*, meaning (in Latin) that the church is always to be in the process of reforming. Sometimes a congregation becomes ineffective in its mission and unfaithful in its confession. Sin continually influences congregations and can divert them from the priorities of God's word and the purposes of God's will. It is in times such as this that God raises up innovative leaders to reform the church so that it better conforms to God's wishes.

A fourth benefit of innovation is that it engenders positive transformation. In fact, some would argue that facilitating positive change is the essence of leadership.[12] It is as lay leaders practice innovation that they exercise a distinctively transformative influence on the congregation.

The key to facilitating innovation is that the new leader is released to do things in his own way. This is where the issue of authority really comes into play. Oftentimes the innovations that develop from the work of the new leader will be difficult for long-tenured leaders to embrace. The former board director, for example, might not fully endorse the initiatives

---

11.   Breen, *Multiplying Missional Leaders*, 84.
12.   Rosabeth Moss Kanter, in the foreword to Lovette Weems, *Church Leadership* (Nashville: Abingdon Press, 2010), ix. See also "Transformational Leadership" in Peter G. Northouse, *Leadership: Theory and Practice* (Los Angeles: Sage, 2010), 171–186.

of his successor. Even the pastor or the professional program staff person may raise eyebrows concerning the innovation. But it must be remembered that if the innovation is within the ends and limitations policies established at the beginning of the process, then that new leader's efforts are within the authority with which he has been vested. Such authorization should be honored. A far better response by the veteran leaders is to affirm the innovation and applaud the new initiative.

SUMMARY

God has entrusted his ministry and mission to the church. The church is composed not only of pastors and professional staff workers. It is composed of all the saints, including lay people who have been gifted for service and called to contribute to the advancement of the gospel. Every baptized believer has been entrusted with gifts to do the Lord's work. That work is done in various contexts, including at home, at work, in neighborhoods, and in the community. But it also is done through the programmatic efforts of the local congregation.

The midsize parish, being a program-oriented organization, provides a fertile environment for lay participation. This involves both a challenge and an opportunity. The challenge is that lay members and visitors must be engaged in order that the medium-sized church not only survives but thrives. The opportunity is that the size culture of medium congregations can be a rich context for "equipping the saints for the work of ministry" (Eph. 4:12).

Critical to the task of engaging lay participants in the work of the congregation is the recruitment of lay leaders. The congregation connects emerging leaders to leadership roles through the process of enlisting. Lay leaders are enlisted from a pool of candidates that includes both veteran volunteers and newcomers to the church. Recruiters persuade them to participate by affirming the importance of the role and by demonstrating that they are needed and qualified for the role. Finally, workers are assured of the congregation's support and appreciation for their leadership.

Lay participation is essential to the vitality of a midsize, program-oriented congregation. Yet even if lay leaders are effectively recruited, this doesn't mean that they are equipped for the task. There also must be an intentional effort to form them into leaders. This process of leadership preparation and empowerment involves instruction, immersion, imitation, and innovation.

This book has emphasized the programmatic orientation of the typical midsize parish. The constituent programs of the congregation require leadership and oversight by the pastor and staff. They also require the participation of the lay members. How are these programs to be initiated and prioritized so that they are truly fruitful? How are the people who lead them to be supported and directed? These are all questions related to the matter of maximizing productivity in the midsize church, the focus of the final chapter.

CHAPTER 10

PRODUCTIVITY

As an officer of Faith Church, Michelle Sanchez participated in the leadership of the congregation. She was amazed at the variety and diversity of programs carried out by her church. At times she was overwhelmed with the complexity of it all. How could she and the other lay officers effectively direct all of these programs? How could these lay leaders work harmoniously with the pastor and professional staff of Faith Church? Most significantly, Michelle wondered how they all might better accomplish the congregation's purposes. Where should the church council invest the congregation's energy and resources to advance Faith Church's mission more effectively?

Michelle turned to her faithful advisor Sally Martin once again. Sally had earlier recommended that the church council identify God's priorities for Faith Church. This led the congregation's leaders to articulate outcomes for its efforts. It became increasingly clear to Michelle that these outcomes would best be accomplished through the varied programs of the church. But how could these be designed and developed to produce the outcomes? This is where Sally's seasoned wisdom might provide guidance.

Michelle welcomed Sally to the table at their favorite coffee shop. "I'm so glad that you can meet with me again, Sally! Your counsel is invaluable." After ordering their lattes the two shared updates of their lives. Then they began discussing Michelle's responsibilities at Faith Church. "I am so impressed with the capable service you are offering your church," Sally affirmed. "God is certainly using you to do his work through your efforts as a congregational leader."

"Thanks for your gracious words," Michelle replied. "But once again I need your help. You know that Faith Church is organized around a number of programs. Although some of these advance the purposes of God's kingdom better than others, I think that they all have a part to play. But it seems to me that they could do better. Currently much of what happens at Faith Church functions routinely. But I believe we need to function more intentionally. I don't think that we are achieving our optimal effectiveness."

Sally reflected and then responded. "It sounds to me that you are concerned that the church's efforts are not reaching their potential productivity. I commend you for having that concern, because it shows that you wish to be a good steward of the ministry potential of this congregation. Even more specifically, it shows that you want Faith Church to bear good fruit through its many programs."

Michelle smiled and replied, "This is why I like talking to you, Sally. You always understand what I'm getting at and even say it better than I do. Yes, the issue is one of fruitfulness. We have lots of programs at our church, but I'm not convinced they are producing optimally. More than that, I don't know how we can start new programs in ways that promote productivity. Any ideas on how to improve that?"

Sally nodded affirmatively. "I do know some ways, and I'm happy to share them with you. Basically it comes down to the productivity of the congregation's ministries and the people who lead them. Let me share what I mean by that."

ACTIVITY AND PRODUCTIVITY

Many midsize churches are active organizations. They are beehives of activity. But activity does not necessarily equate with productivity. People may invest many hours and much energy to the activities of the church and yet miss accomplishing God's priorities. Staff and volunteers may be busily involved in meetings and programs. Yet when all is said and done there is not much mission or ministry resulting from this activity. God calls the church, however, to be productive.

Many will hear that word, *productive*, and deem it to be inappropriate for an ecclesial context. They associate it only with the realm of commerce, business, and manufacturing. Productivity is highly valued in economics. It has to do with the bottom line of business profits. But when it comes to the mission and ministry of the Christian church, some people assume it doesn't fit. In their opinion the church shouldn't get entangled in such worldly pursuits.

However, when properly understood, productivity is appropriate and highly important to the life of the church. It means to deliver the results that the church is commissioned by God to accomplish. In fact, *Webster's New World College Dictionary* provides this definition as the primary sense of the word *productive*: "Producing abundantly, fertile." The secondary sense is to be "marked by abundant production or effective results." Certainly these are salutary goals for a Christian congregation. The association of this term to economics is actually its quaternary sense ("of or engaged in the creating of economic value").[1] Accordingly, it is quite appropriate to apply the words *productive* and *productivity* to the life of the church.

---

1. *Webster's New World Dictionary*, 5th ed., s.v. "productive," accessed December 1, 2017, http://www.yourdictionary.com/productive#websters.

Note how Webster's definition associates productivity with fertility. Thus the primary metaphor applied is an agricultural one. No wonder that when we think of produce our mind images fruit. Similarly, the biblical image best aligned to the concept of productivity is *fruitfulness*. Indeed, being fruitful is a major theme in the Bible.

In the Psalms, fruitfulness is an archetypical image of the results of being rightly oriented toward God (Pss. 1:3; 92:13–14). Yahweh in the Old Testament and Jesus in the New Testament criticized the people of Israel for being unfruitful (Isa. 5:1–7; Matt. 21:19, 43). Jesus calls his followers to bear lasting fruit because it demonstrates discipleship and glorifies God (John 15:8, 16). The Apostle Paul summoned his fellow believers to produce the fruit of mercy, godly character, righteousness, truth, and good works (Rom. 15:28; Gal. 5:22–23; Eph. 5:9; Phil. 1:11; Col. 1:10). Paul refers to new converts as fruit of the church's mission (Rom. 1:13). Many other passages of Scripture utilize this image of fruitfulness as God's desire for his church (Matt. 13:23; Rom. 6:22; 7:4; 2 Cor. 9:10; Phil. 4:17; Col. 1:10; Heb. 12:11; James 3:17).

We have seen that the priorities entrusted to the church are to bring God's gracious *presence* to people who because of sin would be alienated from him, to deliver God's regenerative *power* to those who are spiritually dead or weak, and to advance God's *plan* of restoring the fallen creation, especially fallen humanity. In the Bible, the imagery of fruitfulness is associated with each of these priorities. It is only because Jesus is *present* in people's lives that they become fruitful in God's sight (John 15:4–8; Rom. 7:4; Phil. 1:11). It is only by the Spirit's *power* that sanctified fruit is produced (Ps. 1:3; Rom. 15:13; 1 Cor. 12:3–11; Gal. 5:22–23). It is definitely God's *plan* that his church's mission bears a bumper crop (Matt. 9:37; 13:23; Luke 10:2; John 4:34–37). When the church is focused upon its God-given priorities, fruit abounds!

Of course, we do not inherently have the ability to produce such fruit. The critical prerequisite is to be connected to Christ by faith. It is his presence and power that make this fruit possible! Jesus makes this clear in these words: "Abide in me, and I in you. As the branch cannot bear fruit by itself, unless it abides in the vine, neither can you, unless you abide in me. I am the vine; you are the branches. Whoever abides in me and I in him, he it is that bears much fruit, for apart from me you can do nothing." (John 15:4–6). The fruit we produce is ultimately from him as well as being for him!

This book is about maximizing the effectiveness of the ministry and mission of the midsize church. In assessing this effectiveness, it is wise to focus on fruitfulness. Timothy Keller affirms that fruitfulness is the best theme for evaluating the work of the church:

> As I read, reflected, and taught, I came to the conclusion that a more biblical theme for ministerial evaluation than either success or faithfulness is *fruit-fulness*. . . . Paul spoke of the pastoral nurture of congregations as a form of

gardening. He told the Corinthian Christians they were "God's field" in which some ministers planted, some watered, and some reaped (1 Cor. 3:9). The gardening metaphor shows that both success and faithfulness by themselves are insufficient criteria for evaluating ministry. Gardeners must be faithful in their work, but they must also be skillful, or the garden will fail. Yet in the end, the *degree* of the success of the garden (or the ministry) is determined by factors beyond the control of the gardener. The level of fruitfulness varies due to "soil conditions" (that is, some groups of people have a greater hardness of heart than others) and "weather conditions" (that is, the work of God's sovereign Spirit) as well. . . . When fruitfulness is our criterion for evaluation, we are held accountable but not crushed by the expectation that a certain number of lives will be changed dramatically under our ministry.[2]

Ministry fruitfulness is a valid principal for assessing ministry effectiveness. Accordingly, in evaluating whether or not the medium congregation is maximally effective, it is appropriate to look at its fruit. Maximizing the midsize church involves maximizing productivity.

PROGRAM PRODUCTIVITY

The previous chapters presented some of the dynamics that characterize the medium-size church: programming, pastoral modes of management and leadership, staffing, and lay leader enlistment and empowerment. These dynamics have significant influence on how the medium congregation operates and functions. Effective leaders of the parish are aware of these dynamics and seek to maximize their productivity and potential for good.

The leadership of the midsize church will want to be proactive when attending to the productivity of the parish's programs. Especially pastors will see that the programmatic activities of the church promote the priorities entrusted to it—to bring God's reconciling *presence* to broken and sinful human beings, to deliver God's life-giving *power* to people so that they live in conformity to his will, and to advance God's *plan* of restoring creation to his *shalom*. In other words, leaders will be very intentional in developing and directing the programs so that they are fruitful. What follows are insights for providing just that kind of productive leadership.

In both developing and assessing the programmatic efforts of the midsize church, it is important to have a baseline. This involves the most important areas of programming for advancing the priorities of gospel-centered ministry. It also entails the minimum programming that members and visitors will expect of a congregation of this size. Although this varies depending on context, the programmatic baseline of a middle-size parish usually addresses the areas of worship, children's ministry,

---

2. Timothy Keller, *Center Church: Doing Balanced, Gospel-Centered Ministry in Your City* (Grand Rapids: Zondervan, 2012), 13–14.

youth ministry, Christian education, and community outreach. Clergy, staff, and lay leaders should work to get these key programs established. What would each of these five baseline programs look like when they are fruitful and productive?

Worship

The programmatic focus on worship centers in music and hospitality. The music effort endeavors to provide competent musical enhancement to the worship services. The music will not always sound highly professional, but the musicians should demonstrate competence.

Most traditional worship services are led by an organ or piano. Since these instruments are most regularly used to lead the church's song, the one playing the keys should be competent and not an amateur. Merely good enough might be acceptable in a small church, but not in a midsize one.

In the case of contemporary worship style there will be a lead musician, usually a keyboardist or guitarist. Consistent competence will be expected here as well. Supplementary musical instruments may be added to these regular musical leaders, and they may be performed by hobby musicians (e.g., a teenager who plays the drums in the high school band). The standards of performance will not be as high for these participants. But it is important to recognize that in the middle-size parish musical mediocrity will be detrimental to the worship life of the church and will not be tolerated by many.

The music program will involve groups of performers such as vocal choirs, instrumental ensembles, and praise bands. It is not expected that every worship service includes a performance of a musical group. These may appear more occasionally. But the addition of such groups, if done well, will greatly enhance the aesthetic quality of worship overall. The sanctuary choir is paramount in this regard. It should include singers from multiple generations—from teenagers to octogenarians—and ideally will perform at least monthly in the traditional service, if a traditional style is regularly offered.

The hospitality team is composed of greeters and ushers. Greeters provide a personal one-on-one welcome to both members and visitors at the beginning of the service, and may distribute the printed worship order and announcement bulletin. They also are available after the service has ended to answer questions and give directions to inquirers. Ushers serve to assist visitors in finding seats in the worship space, in gathering the offerings, in directing worshippers in a prescribed manner for reception of the sacraments, and in attending to special concerns that arise during the service.

The hospitality team should be recruited from members who are winsome and welcoming in their personality. A warm smile goes a long way in making a good first impression as well as a positive ongoing atmosphere of welcome. The team members should be trained to carry out their responsibilities with competence.

Children's Ministry

Although it may not apply in some contexts such as a retirement community, one of the most telling barometers of congregational health is the proportion of active participants in the church who are children. A significant season of life for connecting (or reconnecting) with the church is when one becomes a new parent. Accordingly, when few or no opportunities exist for young children to be nurtured in faith, parents will look elsewhere for a church that they can call their own.

What are the baseline elements of the children's ministry program? First among these is the weekly faith formation event designed especially for children. This could be the Sunday morning education hour, traditionally called Sunday school. Or it could be a weekday afternoon or evening event, such as an Awana club. This can be organized according to grade levels or integrated among age levels, but what is most critical is that its activities engage children's interest. Added to these weekly opportunities are occasional special activities, such as an October Trunk and Treat, an Easter weekend egg hunt, Friday evening movie showings, and a servant event to a nearby nursing home. All of these programs involve a significant amount of organization employing multiple teams of volunteer teachers and workers.

For some congregations, the most significant component of the children's ministry is a Christian day school. This takes an immense amount of investment by the congregation, especially in the case of a private or parochial elementary school. Such a program exacts much commitment and many resources from the church. But it usually pays rich dividends in attracting new members and cultivating relationships between the church and the families, not to mention the fertile context for faith formation among children that it provides. These dynamics are less true in the case of preschools and early childhood centers, but can exist to some degree there as well. However, the development of Christian elementary schools is not common among midsize parishes (preschools are more common), and so should not be considered essential to its baseline programmatic development. What is essential, however, is some form of children's ministry.

Youth Ministry

In most situations it is critical that medium-sized congregations provide viable opportunities for involvement of tweens and teens. In developing a youth program, one place to begin is with the baseline ministry previously described—that directed to children. As younger kids become active in regular classes and occasional events, the groundwork has been laid for continuing activity into junior high and eventually high school. Be aware, however, that developing a strong youth program will not happen overnight! It is often wise to begin with one grade of children and build the program as they progress year by year from middle school into high school.

Although it is beneficial to continue a regular Sunday morning class for these ages, this will not be the core of the youth program. Most likely the most impactful experience for the youth will be in regular gatherings for fellowship, fun, study, discussion, and service. Some teenagers will gravitate more to small groups where they can find appropriate intimacy and support. Others will involve themselves more in occasional special activities and retreats. Still others will find participation in servant events most meaningful. It is not to be expected that all of the young people will be involved in all of the activities. What is important is that every young person in the congregation participates in at least one area of involvement. In these contexts young people can be formed in God's word and supported to live as Christ's disciples in their everyday lives.

Christian Education

In the Great Commission Jesus commanded his followers to make disciples by baptizing and teaching (Matt. 28:19–20). The teaching ministry of the local congregation is divinely mandated and vitally necessary. Accordingly, it is part of the baseline of program development in the midsize church. I have already emphasized the importance of educating children and teenagers in the faith. But graduation from high school does not equate with cessation of education in the faith. The middle-sized parish will provide to members of all ages opportunities for learning and reflection in the matters of faith.

In chapter six a taxonomy of group sizes was described involving small (up to 15 participants), family (15 to 50 participants), and fellowship (50 to 150 participants) size groups. It is rare in a midsize church that an educational offering will enter the fellowship size category, although this is possible if a class or workshop is led by an extraordinarily engaging teacher. But it is common for medium churches to provide classes involving small groups and family-size groups. These groups can be organized around the study of the Bible, of Christian doctrine, and of special issues or current concerns that participants have.

Small groups of fifteen people or less have value in that they will lend themselves to greater participation in discussion by the members. Participants are able to reflect on the implications of their learning with one another, to hold each other accountable to the learning process and its application to life, and to support one another through challenges in living the life of discipleship. These groups function best if facilitated by leaders who are theologically competent and able to involve all participants in discussion.

Groups of fifteen to fifty will be best served by a capable instructor who is well grounded in biblical and doctrinal theology. This teacher should communicate truth in an understandable and interesting manner. These educational venues involving a larger number of participants are excellent contexts for imparting information, but less effective for holding people accountable for application. So sometimes the two size groupings can be integrated, involving a plenary session with the larger group and breakout sessions into the smaller groups. This arrangement might optimize the opportunity for growth both in knowledge and life application.

Developing an education program that involves people in all types of classes requires an intentional process for identifying and equipping members of the congregation who are "able to teach" (2 Tim. 2:2). Certainly the pastor will take a prominent role in teaching the congregational members in various Bible classes, theology courses, life-application series, and catechetical venues. But other gifted members—staff and lay— should also participate in teaching classes that are offered by the church.

Outreach

God is a sending God. He sent his Son into the world to redeem the world. He sent his Spirit to distribute the life-giving merits of Christ's salvific work. And he sends us as well. On the evening of his resurrection Jesus announced to his disciples: "As the Father has sent me, even so I am sending you" (John 20:21). Then he breathed on them the Holy Spirit. This is God's purpose—that his church, the body of Christ in the world, be his agency for bringing reconciliation and restoration to a lost and sinful race by the power of his Spirit. He includes us in his mission. Every member of his church, including every member of the midsize church, is called to be a missionary (Matt. 28:16–20; Mark 16:15; Luke 24:46–49; Acts 1:8; Rom. 10:14–17; 1 Peter 2:9–10; 3:15–17).

Accordingly, an essential baseline activity of the medium-sized congregation is that of missional outreach. Oftentimes this moves people into areas that are beyond their comfort zones. That is good. For we are not called to be comfortable, but to be committed to Christ's mission.

Some common ways in which Christian congregations engage their communities and send members abroad are through service programs, servant events, and short-term mission trips.

Service programs are ongoing ministries that address the spiritual and physical needs of the congregation's neighborhood and surrounding community. This includes activities such as hospitality for the homeless, recycling clothing and home goods for the needy, providing language and life skills classes to immigrants, and hosting after-school care for children from the nearby public elementary school.

Servant events involve occasional initiatives of the church to serve the community. Activities in this category might involve a congregation-wide cleanup day in the local park, an afternoon of raking leaves in the yards of elderly and disabled neighbors, or an effort to renovate the house of a homeowner in need.

Short-term mission trips involve teams of congregational members who travel to other cultures and spend one to three weeks repairing a school, leading a basketball camp, teaching vacation Bible school, or digging a well for the citizens of that community. As the opportunity presents itself in all of these contexts—service programs, servant events, mission trips—the missionaries will share the love of Christ not only by their actions but also in their words as they impart the message of the gospel.

An emerging approach to facilitating outreach by congregations is through missional communities. These groups are composed of people who are united around a common cause of service and witness to a particular neighborhood or network of relationships. Reggie McNeal provides the following description of missional communities: "These clusters are larger than cells or small groups, mostly settling in between twenty and thirty participants. They build Christian community on days, at times, and in places that suit the group but are quite distinct from Sunday services. These clusters gain identity and purpose from a united mission vision that might be geographical or network-focused. They are also linked by a network of support and accountability to other midsize groups."[3] Missional communities are often characterized by the inclusion of non-members and even non-Christians in the missional effort. This enables unbelievers to participate in and observe the efforts to serve others, which also becomes a rich context for them to hear the reason for this service—the gospel.

Although outreach is the fifth of five baseline programmatic emphases of the church presented in this chapter, this does not mean it is the least of them or optional in any sense. It is not a supplementary activity.

Nor should the outreach effort be placed in a silo that is separated from the other emphases. Granted, it is appropriate to provide programs distinctively designed to engage the community beyond the walls of the church with the living Christ. But it is equally important to integrate the task of missional outreach into the other areas of programmatic emphasis. For example, the sanctuary choir can occasionally sing in a nearby senior living center. The children's ministry could include opportunities for the children to participate in community service events. The youth ministry might involve teenagers in servant events in the local community and short-term mission trips abroad. The adult education offerings will make participants aware of their missional responsibilities and will train them to be missionaries in their various vocations in life. In each of these cases mission is integrated into the life of all of the programs of the congregation.

Baseline Basics

These are the five baseline ministry areas that ordinarily a middle-sized church will focus on for maximum program productivity: worship (with special concern for music), children's ministry, youth ministry, Christian education, and outreach. Ideally, the congregation will give attention to the development of all five simultaneously. Sometimes it is best to focus on one or two at a time, in which case the congregational leaders

---

3. McNeal, *Missional Renaissance*, 63.

will discern which programs require immediate attention and which can wait. In some contexts one or two of these five prescribed baseline program areas may not be a priority. For example, in a congregation serving predominantly retired people, the emphasis on children's ministry and youth outreach is not appropriate, whereas a program for elderly daycare may be a pressing need.

The main issue is that the congregation's members, guided by the pastor and lay leaders, will seek to discern the distinctive vocation that God has entrusted to that assembly. When this is discovered, then a core of programs may be developed to carry out that calling and in turn to bear fruit for God's kingdom.

EXPANDING PRODUCTIVITY

After the programmatic foundation is laid with the baseline programs, other emphases may be added as the need arises and the resources are available. Such initiatives arise in response to opportunities in the congregation and the community. These ministries are aimed at addressing human needs both of the body and the soul. They arise organically and almost spontaneously and can produce remarkable fruit for God's kingdom.

Expansion from the Middle Out

One way in which these initiatives can be developed is through the official leadership structure of the congregation. This means that the elected leaders serve as the catalysts for developing needed efforts. Usually this takes place within the context of the organizational structure of the church, specifically its boards. It is not without reason that these are referred to as *program* boards. Accordingly, the Board of Christian Education will initiate programs for enhancing the faith life of the congregation's members through instructional classes and educational workshops. The Board of Outreach will organize missional communities and servant events to the neighborhood. The board that oversees children's ministry will attend to programs such as Sunday school, vacation Bible school, and parenting classes. In this sense the initiation of program development can be viewed as deriving from the top–down, although a more accurate way of describing it is from the middle-out, as originally articulated by Gary McIntosh.[4] This means that much productive change in midsize churches originates with the key program boards and teams.

The pastors, program staff, and lay board leaders of middle-sized congregations should constantly ask the question, "What is most needed by our members and by our surrounding community?" These needs will be both of the body and the soul—physical and spiritual needs. They

---

4. McIntosh, *One Size Doesn't Fit All*, 97–110. The *middle-out* dynamic of change that is distinctive to the medium church was discussed in chapter 6, "Programs."

should ultimately address the priorities of the church: to bear the presence of God that reconciles sinners, to deliver the power of God that regenerates unbelievers and reinforces believers, and to accomplish the plan of God to restore his fallen creation. But in identifying which needs are to be addressed in the programmatic efforts of the church, discernment is essential. No congregation, including the midsize one, is able to be all things to all people. No parish is able to do all things to address all needs. Priorities must be made based on the calling of God, the culture of the congregation, the giftedness of the people, and the resources available.

Expansion from the Bottom-Up

Another important way for these programs to be initiated is not from the top down, or even the middle-out, but from the bottom up. This means that the clergy, professional staff, and elected lay leaders are not the catalysts of the new programs, as is the case with the baseline ministries. Instead, lay members who are not elected to any official position in the church initiate these efforts. Each of these becomes a grassroots initiated project that nevertheless is accountable to the pastor, staff, and lay leadership. Such an approach to program development is both organic and spontaneous. It also cultivates a permission-giving ethos in the congregation and a broader sense of ownership of the ministry by the members.

The bottom-up approach involves cultivating an ethos of initiative among the grassroots of the congregation. Everyday disciples are invited to respond to opportunities for mission and ministry of which they become aware. They are encouraged to take responsibility in developing efforts that serve the body of Christ and the community around the congregation. These grassroots initiatives are conducted in the name of the church, but also under its supervision.

This approach is carried out as follows. First, a member of the church identifies a need that she believes can be met through a programmatic initiative. This could be the need for a prayer network, or for a support group for single parents, or for a ministry to assist immigrants who are being settled in the community. For an example, consider a young mother, Claire, whose third child is now two years old. This mom has no extended family members nearby and experienced the challenge of caring for her infant children much on her own. She remembers the difficulties of taking care of infants especially during the first few weeks after birth, and she thinks that the church should provide assistance to new moms by delivering meals to their families. So Claire approaches her pastor and demands that something be done about this. In other words, she expects the pastor to develop a program to aid women who are caring for infants.

At this point the pastor has options for action. One option is to take on the responsibility and see that a program is developed. In this case the pastor researches the problem, designs a plan for implementation, and executes the program. Many pastors see this as their responsibility. However, this is problematic because the pastor's time and energy is limited, so there is a good chance that the program won't get off the ground. Furthermore, this approach creates a culture of dependency among the members; they expect the pastor to do all the work. This option is a top-down approach.

A second option is for the pastor to delegate the development of the program to a program board or staff worker whose area of responsibility aligns with this need. In the case of Claire's idea it is probably the board (or staff worker) responsible for family ministry to which the issue would be delegated. That may work well, but the message conveyed is that only the appointed boards or professional staff workers can make things happen in the church. This option is the middle-out approach.

The third option, the bottom-up one, is for the pastor to encourage Claire to tackle the need. She is directed to spearhead an effort to develop and implement an initiative to help moms of newborns. This empowers her and prevents the development of a culture of dependency on the clergy or professional staff. However, Claire is not left on her own. The pastor responds in a way that provides help and guidance to Claire.

How is this bottom-up process conducted? First, the person originating the grassroots initiative is to gather and organize a working team that will develop the project. This is ideal because she recognizes the need and should have passion to address it. If the one requesting that something be done about a need is unwilling to invest herself in the effort, there is a good likelihood that others will not be so compelled. But if the person is willing to spearhead this initiative, already she demonstrates commitment and passion for the endeavor. In the case of Claire, she is willing to take on this cause, and she does so with zeal and a sense of calling. She connects with other mothers, both young and old, in her network of friendships in the church. She recruits four other women to assist in the effort to develop a program to assist moms of newborns.

Second, if the church is to endorse, support, and publicize this initiative, the initiating team must be accountable to the authority structure of the congregation. That is, the initiating lay members must meet with the appropriate overseeing board or staff member. In the case of Claire, she and her team meet with the children's ministry board to discuss the design and execution of this project that they are calling Mothers Offering Meal Support (MOMS). This connection with the board provides both a line of accountability from the MOMS to the authority structure in the congregation and a means of oversight for the congregation.

Worth the Risk

There are admittedly risks associated with this approach to grassroots initiated programs. Congregation leaders should be aware of these, but not intimidated by them.

The first potential hazard is that the new program is not aligned with the priorities established by the church as a whole. The greatest peril is that the initiative actually moves in an opposing direction from the larger strategic direction that has been embraced by the congregation. This would mean that this program will work at odds with the strategic momentum of the congregation, and thus reduce it. Rarely is such a problem the case, but it can happen. More likely the initiative is not completely at odds with the agreed-upon mission, but it is also not demonstrably supportive of it. The danger here is that valuable resources of time, effort, and money will be expended on one program at the expense of others that might contribute more fully to the forward motion of the parish. As a result, the corporate energy of the congregation becomes diffused.

This problem, however, can be avoided. At the very beginning of the conversation the initiating group is instructed to demonstrate that its efforts align with the stated strategic purposes and priorities of the church. The board officer or staff worker meets with the leaders of the initiative to discuss the vision of the congregation and to assess how the new effort might contribute to that. This helps all of the programs of the church to remain roughly aligned to the strategic priorities that have been approved by the whole.

A second risk is that the spontaneously generated initiative will become maverick and unhealthy, even if its objectives are ostensibly in line with the congregation's strategic direction. This can happen when false doctrine emerges in the group. It also occurs when relational strife arises among members in the team or between the group's membership and others outside of it. Less frequently it can be manifest as a moral or ethical failure that is tolerated in the group and that runs contrary to the will of God.

Because of these potential pitfalls, even before a grassroots initiative is endorsed by the overseeing agency in the church, the initiating group should be informed that the board or staff person has the right to step in if such problems arise. The representative of the official congregational leadership could speak as follows: "The children's ministry board is responsible to oversee everything related to care for children and their parents undertaken in the name of this congregation. We take seriously what the Bible says about Christians practicing sound doctrine and living at peace with each other. Accordingly, our board reserves the right to intervene in any program under its purview that may evidence doctrinal error, unethical or immoral behavior, and malice among its members."

My experience is that rarely does such drastic action need to be taken, especially in the scale of congregational interaction typical of the midsize church. Nonetheless, this safeguard is helpful in preventing spontaneously generated programs from doing more harm than good in the parish. It increases the likelihood that what is produced by the group is good fruit, not bad.

PRIORITIZING FOR PRODUCTIVITY

The programmatic nature of the midsize parish provides potential for vital engagement in ministry within and mission beyond the walls of the church. But there are perils as well. One peril is that the multiplicity of initiatives facilitates not the business of God but the busyness of members without much fruitfulness. Another peril is that the efforts become disintegrated from each other, and even adversely independent, so that "everyone does what is right in his own eyes" (cf. Judg. 21:25). A third pitfall is that the church becomes overextended in terms of its human resources and thus participants become frustrated and exhausted. This is why it is critical that the leaders of the medium church provide true leadership by prioritizing and aligning the activities of the church. Indeed, the process of developing initiatives and supporting them itself should be strategic.

The first place to begin in attending to prioritization is to consider the divine priorities, that is, those premier commitments that God has entrusted to his church. These are summarized as bearing God's gracious *presence* to needy sinners, delivering God's life-giving *power* for new life in Christ, and joining in God's *plan* of restoring what is fallen to God's intended design. These outcomes must guide the initiation and execution of all of the efforts of the church. Activities of the church that minister to human needs must contribute to the advancement of God's work of the gospel. Congregational programs—whether they be baseline, middle-out, or grassroots in origin—must serve God's priorities of reconciling sinners to himself and restoring the fallen creation to flourish in his grace. These are the areas of ministry upon which the parish focuses energy and talents.

The insights of Thom Rainer and Eric Geiger are useful in guiding a congregation to prioritize its efforts in order to be more productive. In their book, *Simple Church*, the authors advocate a process for de-cluttering the church's system of activities and then to align them to the mission of God. Rainer and Geiger propose four qualities of a simple church that demonstrate a streamlined process for discipleship: clarity (clearly identifying and committing to goals and priorities), movement (designing the ministry process to move people toward the priorities), alignment (unifying around the same approach to the discipleship process by following a shared ministry roadmap), and focus (saying yes to whatever advances the priorities of the church and no to those efforts that distract from such aligned movement). This book is worthy of consultation for help in prioritizing the efforts of the midsize church.[5]

---

5. Thom Rainer and Eric Geiger, *Simple Church: Returning to God's Process for Making Disciples* (Nashville: B&H Publishing, 2006).

Signature Programs

Related to the process of prioritizing activities is the attempt to develop one, two, or three of these as signature efforts of the church. A signature is an identifying characteristic or mark, such as a handwritten autograph. The signature is integral to one's identity. So also a few key efforts in the parish can serve as identifying marks of that congregation. Gary McIntosh recommends that a midsize congregation in particular undertake to develop select signature ministries that promote its distinctive identity. "Medium churches need to build on their key ministries to form a distinct identity in the community. Studies have found that healthy churches of this size usually have at least one ministry for which they are legendary in their community."[6] The signature effort of one congregation might be its excellent Christian day school. For another it might be the ministry to teenagers. Another church might be known in the community for its extraordinary music program that contributes to an inspiring worship experience. In each case, the congregation's identity becomes closely associated with the signature effort.

Having one strong signature ministry will bring great benefit to a midsize church. Yet ideally, a medium-size congregation will have more than one key effort. Kennon Callahan, in his book on effective congregations, affirms that a healthy congregation will have one strong outreach effort that endeavors to serve the community beyond the membership and one key internal program that provides significant care to the members.[7] The point is that the emphasis is not *either-or*. It is not the option of *either* a signature outreach initiative *or* a key internal ministry. A vibrant congregation will undertake to cultivate both kinds of efforts in a balanced attempt to make an impact in the lives of its members and in the lives of others.

The signature *outreach effort* will be missional in its orientation. It is driven to serve primarily those who are in the neighborhood or community surrounding the church building. The location of activity is not usually in the church building, but beyond. In this case, the congregation's members are *sent* to bring the restorative *shalom* of God to others. The direction of movement is centrifugal—from the inside out. The effort's participants, and potentially even some of its leaders, include both congregational members and non-members from the community. Examples of this type of signature mission would be activities that involve people in the following ways:

- A rotation of volunteers who regularly serve evening meals to children at a nearby public school and offer tutoring services to them.

---

6. McIntosh, *One Size Doesn't Fit All*, 150.
7. Kennon Callahan, *Twelve Keys to an Effective Church: Strategic Planning for Mission* (San Francisco: Jossey-Bass Publishers, 2010), 149.

- An outreach to widows and widowers in the community that provides grief counseling through a system of support groups.
- Sports camps and athletic leagues for teenagers and young adults in the community that include an emphasis on the stewardship of one's body and spirit.
- Work teams that periodically clean the neighborhood by picking up trash on the streets and on public property and by removing graffiti.

The signature *internal program* will be ministry oriented. It is driven to serve primarily those who are already members of the church. The locus of activity is frequently in the church building. In this case, the congregation's members are *gathered* to bring the restorative *shalom* of God to one another. The direction of movement is centripetal—pulling inward. The internal program's participants and leaders are primarily congregational members who care for and serve each other. Examples of this type of signature ministry would be programs that involve members in the following ways:

- A music program uses the musical talents of the church's members in multiple choirs, praise bands, wind ensembles, brass quartets, and the like.
- A vibrant catechetical curriculum forms the faith of members from childhood to adulthood.
- A program of caregiving such as the Stephen Ministry® model trains members to do visitation to those in the congregation who suffer grief, loneliness, and trauma.

Callahan contends that the best combination of signature programs will result in each complementing the other.[8] The outreach effort and the internal ministry are connected by some element of common ground or of mutual interest. For example, a catechetical program for children (which is primarily internally oriented) has a common interest with the mission outreach to provide tutoring to kids in the nearby public school in that both are concerned with the education of children. A congregation with strong signature programs such as these would be recognized in the community as having a commitment to teaching children.

Another way to develop the signature efforts of the church is to focus on the existing programs that demonstrate the greatest effectiveness in accomplishing the parish's priorities. Gary McIntosh applies the Pareto Principle to this approach (i.e., that twenty percent of effort accomplishes eighty percent of priorities). In this scenario, the congregational leaders do an audit of the results from each of the church's programs. The twenty percent of the programs that demonstrate the most effectiveness in advancing the priorities of the church are the ones that are given the most attention and

---

8. Ibid., 156–57.

resources by the leaders of the congregation. This results in better stewarding of the congregation's human resources, talent pool, and finances.[9]

The Quality Quotient

The development of a few signature efforts requires a focus on elevating the quality of those key programs. If the program doesn't demonstrate excellence in its execution and results, it can hardly be regarded as exemplary. So the attainment of a high degree of quality in the one, two, or three signature efforts of a midsize church is critical.

But that does not mean that a concern for quality can be neglected in the other programmatic efforts of the program church. Compared to the small congregation, people will have much higher expectations for what is offered by the midsize parish. Timothy Keller explains this difference thus: "The medium-sized church will also grow as it multiplies classes, groups, services, and ministries, but the key to medium-sized growth is improving the quality of the ministries and their effectiveness to meet real needs. The small church can accommodate amateurish quality because the key attraction is its intimacy and family-like warmth. But the medium-sized church's ministries must be different. Classes really must be great learning experiences. Music must meet aesthetic needs. Preaching must inform and inspire."[10]

In addition to my position as a seminary professor, I currently serve as a pastor of a small church. The worship attendance at this church averages about 40 people each Sunday. The congregation cannot afford a full-time pastor, and that is why I serve part-time. In this small family-sized congregation, relationships are supremely significant. The members love one another and care for each other. They refer to each other as being part of the family. This is a great strength of this congregation. But it also allows for lower expectations regarding the quality of the church's offerings. For example, occasionally there is no organist available for a given worship service. In those situations I serve as the accompanying musician who plunks away grievously at the piano. Believe me, this is about as low a level of quality as one can tolerate! But the point is that in a mid-size church this wouldn't be tolerated, and well it shouldn't! It is acceptable in a small church, because the members are there on account of their relationships with each other, not because the music program is great. But it is not acceptable in a medium-sized parish. A much higher level of quality is expected of all efforts, especially those that impact the corporate worship service. The production of good fruit in the midsize church means that by quality standards it really must be *good*!

Visitors to a midsize church will assess their attraction to that church primarily on the basis of the quality of its worship services and the programs

---

9.   McIntosh, *One Size Doesn't Fit All*, 121–22.

10.   Keller, *Leadership and Church Size Dynamics*, 10.

offered, not on the basis of relationships. Even existing members will make a similar assessment, although perhaps to a lesser degree. For a middle-sized parish to attract and retain members, it will need to give attention to the quality of all that is done in its name. Since the midsize church is by its nature program-oriented, it is especially important to notch up the quality of the programs offered. This should certainly be the case with the few signature efforts that contribute to the identity of the congregation. Next in importance are the baseline ministries. Quality control must be maintained in these as well, and frequently in this order of priority: worship, children's ministries, and outreach.

PROPERTY AND PRODUCTIVITY

Related to the issue of quality is the resource of facilities. With the exception perhaps of visitation and some outreach-oriented efforts, the church delivers many of its activities within the walls of its physical plant. Accordingly, for the program to demonstrate a high degree of quality the physical place in which it is held must also be perceived as being clean, attractive, comfortable, up-to-date, and well-maintained. Admittedly, most churches of all sizes are challenged with updating and maintaining facilities. And usually the financial resources of the congregation are not adequate to satisfy everyone's dreams for what the facilities might be. Nonetheless, leaders of midsize parishes should make every effort to be good stewards of the physical plant by keeping it well maintained and attractive and by maximizing its usefulness.

As a medium congregation expands its programmatic offerings, the demand for physical space to house these activities will also increase. Due to limited finances, frequently the church will not be able to construct additional buildings. Trying to fit all the activities into the existing building can be quite a challenge! But it is a challenge addressed with creative thinking. The most reasonable solution to this pressure is to designate much of the space in the building as multi-use. It is less productive to designate a given space for only a single function. For example, classes that are used by the preschool during the daytime hours of the week can be used for Sunday school or special children's events on the weekend or even for support groups that meet in the evening. A foyer designated for fellowship before and after worship services on Sunday could be used for the gathering of the women's auxiliary on Tuesday and the youth group on Thursday. The point is to maximize the utility of the space by designating it as multi-use.

No doubt this will eventually lead to turf wars between groups that utilize the same space at different times. Thus the leadership will be vigilant in coordinating these activities and in helping participants to share space with an attitude of cooperation rather than competition.

Although the middle-sized church may gather in a modestly designed and furnished building, every effort should be made to keep that space updated and attractive. This is where quality control and the commitment to excellence especially come into play. At the very minimum, the physical plant must be clean. Dirt, grime, and mold are real turn-offs to people.

Next, although the building may not be new, it should be well maintained. This means it is regularly painted, both in terms of exterior trim and interior walls. Someone who has talent for interior decorating should select paint so that dated colors are not applied to the walls but they look fresh and contemporary. Floor coverings—carpeting, tile, wood, laminate—should similarly be updated periodically in order to maintain a contemporary appearance. Comfort systems providing heating and air conditioning should equal the quality of what most people experience in their homes and workplaces. The parish should prioritize cleaning and updating bathrooms, especially those accessed by visitors and parents with small children.

Finally, technology is an integral aspect of everyday life in the twenty-first century. So the church's technology resources must be up-to-date. High definition electronic screens, digital sound systems, smart AV equipment, and wireless internet availability should replace outmoded forms of technology within the church facility.

Bricks and mortar, sparkling clean restrooms, attractive décor, Wi-Fi access—these are not the essence of ministry. But they support the ministry of the church. They are resources that enhance the church's mission. Most importantly, they impact fruitfulness. Of course, a congregation may have new facilities and the latest technology and still not be productive for God's kingdom. Yet we dare not promote a false dichotomy between the physical and the spiritual. Leaders of medium churches who seek to maximize productivity will attend to both.

A FINAL WORD OF HOPE

This book has as its purpose to help leaders of middle-sized congregations to guide those churches so that they may reach their maximum productivity in mission and ministry. It is directed to pastors, staff workers, and lay leaders who wish to optimize the impact of these parishes for good. There are many prescriptions, proscriptions, and practices that are presented in these pages. Methods, modes, and measures are commended. There are diagnoses and directions. All of these have been offered in the hope of benefiting you, the leader of the medium-size church.

I recognize that such prescriptions can be overwhelming. It may appear from these pages that the effort to maximize the midsize church involves maximum skill and energy. Borrowing a line from the Apostle Paul, you may be inclined to ask, "Who is sufficient for these things?" (2 Cor. 2:16). The fact is, in our own strength none of us is sufficient, especially when it comes to accomplishing the core priorities of the church: to bear God's gracious *presence* into the lives of sinful people, to deliver God's *power* to restore and enrich life among those he loves, and to advance God's *plan* to care for the wellbeing of his human creatures and all of creation.

The good news is that we do not need to be sufficient for such things in our own strength. For it is in the strength of the Lord that we are made strong. The same gospel power that we deliver to others in mission and ministry is the power that energizes and sustains us in the journey. Paul recognized this reality acutely when he wrote, "Such is the confidence that we have through Christ toward God. Not that we are sufficient in ourselves to claim anything as coming from us, but our sufficiency is from God, who has made us competent to be ministers of a new covenant, not of the letter but of the Spirit" (2 Cor. 3:4–6).

Indeed, our sufficiency is in God! He is the one who has called us to lead his people. He is the one who makes us competent for his gospel ministry by imbuing us with the gospel itself. He is the one who through his word and sacraments sustains and enlivens us for the difficult task of shepherding his flock. Who is sufficient for these things? God is. And by his grace he makes us competent to maximize the ministry of the midsize church.

PASSAGES

God calls many Christian congregations to function in the capacity of medium-size. This is their vocation. God uses various sizes of Christian congregations to advance his kingdom—small, medium, large. The Lord is no respecter of size when it comes to churches. Any size of congregation—including the middle-sized church—can effectively carry out the mission and ministry God entrusts to it.

The previous chapters will help you to guide a midsize church to achieve the highest level of effectiveness possible given its distinctive size culture and dynamics. You can celebrate the unique characteristics of a medium-sized church. You should capitalize on those characteristics for the sake of the gospel. You are now able to maximize the potential for fruitful mission and ministry of the medium-sized church you lead. Whatever your role—pastor, staff worker, lay leader, or lay member—the middle-sized congregation you serve can benefit from your leadership as it is guided by insights from this book.

But a midsize congregation does not always remain that size. Sometimes the number of its participants increases, creating a large church. Sometimes its membership decreases so that it becomes a small church. Such transitions can be traumatic and troubling to the saints who gather there. What are some resources for promoting a healthy size transition? How can congregations experience such passages in peace?

The purpose of this book is not to guide church leaders in making these transitions. Its purpose is to maximize effectiveness within the size culture of the medium church, not necessarily to coach leaders to navigate through the change from one size to another. There are other books and resources that serve this purpose, and do so ably. For pastors and parish leaders who find themselves in such transitions, or who seek intentionally to move through these transitions, other resources are here commended for your consideration.

The Alban Institute has given attention to the matter of church size transitions. Two resources address this subject thoroughly. *The In-between Church: Navigating Size Transitions in Congregations* provides a general orientation to the dynamics of transitioning from one size culture to another.[1] The second resource, *Size Transitions in Congregations,* is a compendium of essays written by fourteen contributors. These essays address the dynamics that accompany various size passages: small to midsize, midsize to large, large to midsize, midsize to small. They provide helpful guidance to congregations that are confronting these varied size transitions.

Gary McIntosh has written two books that guide congregations to make the transitions from small to midsize and from midsize to large: *One Size Doesn't Fit All,* and *Taking Your Church to the Next Level.* McIntosh is the president of the Church Growth Network, and so he is a promoter of size growth in congregations. His books help congregations to cultivate attitudes and practices conducive to church growth. McIntosh's two resources also identify some distinctive dynamics and proactive strategies that congregations will likely need to address in order to successfully navigate the transitions from small to medium to large.

FROM SMALL TO MEDIUM

Two resources are particularly valuable in assisting congregations successfully to navigate the passage from a small church (pastoral size) to a medium congregation (program size). Alice Mann addresses this specific transition in her book, *Raising the Roof: The Pastoral-to-Program Size Transition.* Similarly, Kevin Martin provides a practical guidebook through this passage in his work entitled *The Myth of the 200 Barrier: How to Lead through Transitional Growth.* And certainly any leader of a small church who wishes to help a parish move into and inhabit the size culture of a medium church can benefit from the insights provided in the book you are now holding.

FROM MEDIUM TO LARGE

I am not aware of any book that has as its exclusive purpose to guide leaders through the transition from midsize church to large congregation. However, Susan Beaumont's volume, *Inside the Large Congregation*, identifies the distinctive dynamics and organizational needs of large churches as well as strategies and practices for flourishing within the size culture of the large parish.[2] Clergy and leaders of middle-size churches who aspire to lead their congregations to become large will profit from the book's insights. Chapter three is particularly helpful, in that it compares the characteristics of the midsize church with three size categories associated with large churches.[3]

---

1. Full information for the following books appears earlier in the book or in the bibliography.
2. Beaumont, *Inside the Large Congregation.*
3. Ibid., 43–69.

FROM MEDIUM TO MULTIPLYING

Midsize churches that are growing in membership and attendance may opt to divide and multiply. That is, instead of transitioning to the size culture of a large church, these congregations remain as midsize but choose to birth new churches by sending a significant proportion of members into new church plants. This option has two important benefits. The first is that God's kingdom is expanded by establishing new congregations. The second is that the congregation is spared the difficulty and trauma of attempting to adopt a new size culture (although the process of dividing to form multiple churches certainly can involve some trauma). That is, the congregation remains midsize, but its influence and impact upon the mission of God expands because it multiplies mission posts through the planting of new congregations.

Timothy Keller maintains that planting churches should be a natural and customary practice of *all* Christian congregations, no matter what size.[4] The middle-size church is well positioned for this endeavor. Reflecting on the trend away from large churches among younger generations, the Barna Research Group predicts: "Given the values and goals of people in the two youngest generations—the Busters and Mosaics—we anticipate mid-sized churches becoming a more significant force in the future, with many of those churches spawning new congregations rather than expanding to become megachurches."[5] Numeric growth can be realized by adding members to one congregation. But it can also be achieved by multiplying members by means of multiple sites. Fine resources exist that guide congregations to plant churches, including *The Church Planter's Toolkit; How to Multiply Your Church: The Most Effective Way to Grow God's Kingdom; Church Planter: The Man, the Message, the Mission; First Steps for Planting a Missional Church;* and *Redeemer Church Planting Manual.*[6]

FROM LARGER TO SMALLER

The scenarios for size transition envisioned above all assume numeric growth in congregations. But sometimes this is not the case. Rather than

---

4. Keller, *Center Church*, 355.
5. "Small Churches Struggle to Grow because of the People They Attract," *Barna*. Busters refer to the generation of those born from 1965 to 1983. Mosaics refer to those born after 1983.
6. Robert Logan and Steven Ogne, *The Church Planter's Toolkit: A Self-study Resource Kit for Church Planters and Those Who Supervise Them* (Alta Loma, CA: CRM, 1994); Ralph Moore and Ed Stetzer, *How to Multiply Your Church: The Most Effective Way to Grow God's Kingdom* (Ventura, CA: Regal, 2009); Darrin Patrick, *Church Planter: The Man, the Message, the Mission* (Wheaton, IL: Crossway, 2010); Gary Rohrmayer, *First Steps for Planting a Missional Church* (Lindenhurst, IL: Your Journey Resources, 2006); J. Allen Thompson and Timothy Keller, *Redeemer Church Planting Manual* (New York: Redeemer City to City, 2002).

growth there is decline. Congregations often exhibit a predictable life cycle that resembles a bell curve. This includes a period of decreasing membership and attendance toward the end of the life cycle.[7] Thus it is not uncommon that the passage through which a congregation travels is from larger to smaller in size.

This passage can be from a large church to a medium church, in which case this book can serve as a resource for aiding in the transition. The passage can also be from a midsize parish to becoming a small congregation. The causes for such decline may vary: changing neighborhood, population flight, aging membership, a church conflict or scandal, or an unwillingness to engage in mission. Whatever the cause, pastors and leaders of these churches need help. Useful resources for navigating through transitions of decline are three essays in the book, *Size Transitions*: "Congregations in Decline: How Context Affects Size" by Alice Mann, "When Membership Declines: Letting Go and Moving Forward" by Roy Oswald, and "The Death and Dying of a Congregation: An Experience of God's Grace" by Daphne Burt.[8] A more thorough resource for assisting declining churches to engage the transition in a healthy manner is *Facing Decline, Finding Hope: New Possibilities for Faithful Churches* by Jeffrey Jones.[9]

Churches that transition into becoming small will need to adapt to the size culture of the small church. Two excellent resources for ministry leadership in small congregations are written by Glenn Daman: *Shepherding the Small Church,* and *Leading the Small Church: How to Develop a Transformational Ministry.*[10] Other helpful guides are *The Healthy Small Church* by Dennis Bickers, and *The Strategically Small Church* by Brandon O'Brien.[11]

---

7. McIntosh, *Taking Your Church to the Next Level*, 29–34.

8. Gaede, *Size Transitions in Congregations*, 151–69.

9. Jeffrey Jones, *Facing Decline, Finding Hope: New Possibilities for Faithful Churches* (Lanham, MD: Rowman & Littlefield, 2015).

10. Daman, Glenn C., *Shepherding the Small Church* (Grand Rapids: Kregel Publications, 2nd ed., 2007); Daman, Glenn C., *Leading the Small Church: How to Develop a Transformational Ministry* (Grand Rapids: Kregel Publications, 2006).

11. Bickers, Dennis, *The Healthy Small Church: Diagnosis and Treatment for the Big Issues* (Kansas City: Beacon Hill Press, 2005); O'Brien, Brandon, *The Strategically Small Church: Intimate, Nimble, Authentic, and Effective* (Bloomington, MN: Bethany House, 2010).

BIBLIOGRAPHY

The Barna Group. "Small Churches Struggle to Grow Because of the People They Attract." Last Modified September 2, 2003. https://www.barna.com/research/small-churches-struggle-to-grow-because-of-the-people-they-attract/.

Beaumont, Susan. *Inside the Large Congregation*. Herndon, VA: The Alban Institute, 2011.

Bennethum, D. M. *Listen! God is Calling!: Luther Speaks of Vocation, Faith, and Work*. Minneapolis: Augsburg Fortress, 2003.

Bickers, Dennis. *The Healthy Small Church: Diagnosis and Treatment for the Big Issues*. Kansas City: Beacon Hill Press, 2005.

Breen, Mike. *Multiplying Missional Leaders: From Half-hearted Volunteers to a Mobilized Kingdom Force*. Pawleys Island, SC: 3 Dimension Ministries, 2012.

Callahan, Kennon. *Twelve Keys to an Effective Church: Strong, Healthy Congregations Living in the Grace of God*. 2nd ed. San Francisco: Jossey-Bass Publishers, 2010.

Chavez, Mark. *Congregations in America*. Cambridge, MA: Harvard University Press, 2004.

Cooperative Congregations Studies Partnership. "Faith Communities Today Frequencies for the Entire Survey Population." *Faith Communities Today 2010 National Survey of Congregations*. Hartford, CT: Hartford Institute for Religion Research, 2011.

Cormode, Scott. *Making Spiritual Sense: Christian Leaders as Spiritual Interpreters*. Nashville: Abingdon Press, 2006.

Daman, Glenn C. *Leading the Small Church: How to Develop a Transformational Ministry*. Grand Rapids: Kregel Publications, 2006.

Daman, Glenn C. *Shepherding the Small Church: A Leadership Guide for the Majority of Today's Churches*. 2nd ed. Grand Rapids: Kregel Publications, 2007.

Dillon, William P. *People Raising: A Practical Guide to Raising Funds*. Chicago: Moody Publishers, 2012.

Dunbar, Robin. "Coevolution of NeoCortical Size, Group Size and Language in Humans." *Behavior and Brain Sciences* 16, no. 4 (1993): 681–735.

Elmore, Tim. *Habitudes: Images that Form Leadership Habits and Attitudes*. Atlanta: Growing Leaders Inc., 2006–2009.

Forrest, Benjamin and Chet Roden, eds. *Biblical Leadership: Theology for the Everyday Leader*. Grand Rapids: Kregel Publications, 2017.

Gaede, Beth Ann, ed. *Size Transitions in Congregations*. Herndon, VA: The Alban Institute, 2001.

Galvin, James. *I've Got Your Back: A Leadership Parable*. Elgin, IL: Tenth Power, 2012.

Hunter, James Davison. *To Change the World: The Irony, Tragedy, and Possibility of Christianity in the Late Modern World*. New York: Oxford University Press, 2010.

Jones, Jeffrey. *Facing Decline, Finding Hope: New Possibilities for Faithful Churches*. Lanham, MD: Rowman & Littlefield Publishers, 2015.

Keller, Timothy. *Center Church: Doing Balanced, Gospel-Centered Ministry in Your City*. Grand Rapids: Zondervan, 2012.

Keller, Timothy. *Every Good Endeavor: Connecting Your Work to God's Work*. New York: Penguin Books, 2014.

Keller, Timothy. *Leadership and Church Size Dynamics: How Strategy Changes with Growth*. New York: Redeemer City to City, 2010.

Kobs, Matthew. "Technology and Community." In *Inviting Community*, edited by Robert Kolb and Theodore Hopkins, 179–193. St. Louis: Concordia Seminary Press, 2013.

Kotter, John. *Leading Change*. Boston: Harvard Business School Press, 2012.

Kouzes, James, and Barry Z. Posner, eds. *Christian Reflections on the Leadership Challenge*. San Francisco: Jossey-Bass, 2004.

Mann, Alice. *The In-Between Church: Navigating Size Transitions in Congregations*. Herndon, VA: The Alban Institute, 1998.

Mann, Alice. *Raising the Roof: The Pastoral-to-Program Size Transition*. Herndon, VA: The Alban Institute, 2001.

Martin, Kevin. *The Myth of the 200 Level*. Nashville: Abingdon Press, 2005.

McIntosh, Gary. *One Size Doesn't Fit All: Bringing Out the Best in Any Size Church*. Grand Rapids: Fleming H. Revell, 2006.

McIntosh, Gary. *Staff Your Church for Growth: Building Team Ministry in the 21st Century*. Grand Rapids: Baker Books, 2000.

McIntosh, Gary. *Taking Your Church to the Next Level: What Got You Here Won't Get You There*. Grand Rapids: Baker Books, 2009.

McNeal, Reggie. *Missional Renaissance: Changing the Scorecard for the Church*. San Francisco: Jossey-Bass, 2009.

Miller, Herb. *Church Effectiveness Nuggets, Volume 18: Navigating toward Maximum Effectiveness in Midsize Churches*. N.p.: Herb Miller, 2009.

Miller, Herb. *Church Effectiveness Nuggets, Volume 28: Coaching Midsize Congregations toward Positive Change*. N.p.: Herb Miller, 2009.

Moore, Ralph, and Ed Stetzer. *How to Multiply Your Church: The Most Effective Way to Grow God's Kingdom*. Ventura, CA: Regal, 2009.

Newport, Frank. "Three-Quarters of Americans Identify as Christian." *Gallup News*, December 24, 2014. Accessed November 1, 2017. http://www.gallup.com/poll/180347/three-quarters-americans-

identify-christian.aspx?utm_source=RELIGION_AND_SOCIAL_
TRENDS&utm_medium=topic&utm_campaign=tiles.

Newton, Phil. *The Mentoring Church: How Pastors and Congregations
Cultivate Leaders*. Grand Rapids: Kregel Publishing, 2017.

Northouse, Peter G. *Leadership: Theory and Practice*. 5th ed. Los Angeles:
Sage Publications, 2010.

O'Brien, Brandon. *The Strategically Small Church: Intimate, Nimble,
Authentic, and Effective*. Bloomington, MN: Bethany House, 2010.

Oswald, Roy. *Making Your Church More Inviting*. Herndon, VA: The Alban
Institute, 1992.

Patrick, Darrin. *Church Planter: The Man, the Message, the Mission*.
Wheaton, IL: Crossway, 2010.

Peter, David. "The Challenge of Church Membership in the Twenty-First
Century: Old and New Directions." In *Inviting Community*, edited by
Robert Kolb and Theodore Hopkins, 159–177. St. Louis: Concordia
Seminary Press, 2013.

Preus, Jacob III. "The Holy Ministry and the Holy Priesthood: The Gospel
Office and the Office from the Gospel." *Concordia Journal* 24, no. 3
(1998): 36–42.

Putnam, Robert. *Bowling Alone: The Collapse and Revival of American
Community*. New York: Simon and Schuster, 2000.

Rainer, Thom, and Eric Geiger. *Simple Church: Returning to God's Process
for Making Disciples*. Nashville: B&H Publishing, 2006.

Rardin, Richard. *The Servant's Guide to Leadership*. Brentwood, PA: Selah
Publishing, 2001.

Rohrmayer, Gary. *First Steps for Planting a Missional Church*. Lindenhurst,
IL: Your Journey Resources, 2006.

Routhage, Arlin. *Sizing Up a Congregation for New Member Ministry*. New
York: Seabury Press, 1983.

Schaller, Lyle. *The Middle Sized Church: Problems and Prescriptions*. Nashville: Abingdon Press, 1985.

Schaller, Lyle. *The Multiple Staff and the Larger Church*. Nashville: Abingdon Press, 1980.

Schaller, Lyle. *The Very Large Church: New Rules for Leaders*. Nashville:
Abingdon Press, 2000.

Thompson, J. Allen, and Timothy Keller. *Redeemer Church Planting
Manual*. New York: Redeemer City to City, 2002.

Veith, Gene. *God at Work: Your Christian Vocation in All of Life*. Wheaton,
IL: Crossway, 2011.

Weeks, Louis B. *All for God's Glory: Redeeming Church Scutwork*. Herndon,
VA: The Alban Institute, 2008.

Weems, Lovett H. *Church Leadership: Vision, Team, Culture, and Integrity*.
Rev. ed. Nashville: Abingdon Press, 2010.

Wingren, Gustav. *Luther on Vocation*. Translated by Carl C. Rasmussen.
Evansville, IN: Ballast, 1994.

Woods, Rod. *Freed to Lead: How Your Identity in Christ Can Transform Any Leadership Role*. Grand Rapids: Monarch Books, 2016.

Woolever, Cynthia and Deborah Bruce. *Beyond the Ordinary: Ten Strengths of U.S. Congregations*. Louisville: Westminster John Knox Press, 2004.

INDEX